ALSO FROM THE SAGER GROUP

Miss Havilland: A Novel
by Gay Daly

The Orphan's Daughter: A Novel
by Jan Cherubin

Lifeboat No. 8: Surviving the Titanic
by Elizabeth Kaye

Into the River of Angels: A Novel
by George R. Wolfe

Who She Was: My Search for My Mother's Life
by Samuel G. Freedman

The Stories We Tell: Classic True Tales
by America's Greatest Women Journalists

New Stories We Tell: True Tales by America's New
Generation of Great Women Journalists

Newswomen: Twenty-Five Years of Front-Page Journalism

The Someone You're Not: True Stories of Sports, Celebrity,
Politics & Pornography by Mike Sager

What Makes Sammy Jr. Run?: Classic Celebrity Journalism
Volume 1 (1960s and 1970s) edited by Alex Belth

Our Washington, DC: America's Hometown in Transition
edited by Susan Sheehan

The Dreyfus Collection: A Novel
by Estelle Rubin Brager

See our entire library at TheSagerGroup.net

GRAY SKIES, BLUE LINE

Letters from a Cop

VICTOR LETONOFF

Gray Skies, Blue Line: Letters from a Cop

© 2026 Victor Letonoff

All rights reserved. No part of this publication may be reproduced,
stored in a retrieval system, or transmitted, in any form or by any
means, electronic, mechanical, photocopying, recording, or otherwise,
without the prior written permission of the publisher.
Published in the United States of America.

Cover art, design and interior design by Siori Kitajima, PatternBased.com

Cataloging-in-Publication data for this book
is available from the Library of Congress.

ISBN-13:
eBook: 978-1-958861-97-4
Paperback: 978-1-958861-98-1
Hardcover: 978-1-958861-99-8

Published by The Sager Group LLC
(TheSagerGroup.net)

GRAY SKIES, BLUE LINE

Letters from a Cop

VICTOR LETONOFF

In the days after Ferguson, crowds marched down the street screaming, "What do we want?"
"Dead cops!"
"When do we want it?"
"Now!"
— The Profession, A Memoir of Community, Race, and the Arc of Policing in America, by Bill Bratton

CONTENTS

He seems like a decent-enough fella for a policeman.
— *The Hunter,* by Tana French

1

Letter to the Young Cop's Well-Intentioned Family and Friends

You've got a cop in your life. A son or daughter, your spouse, your brother-in-law, your neighbor across the street. You're proud of your cop, and though you may not see eye-to-eye politically, you know — and you tell people this whenever you mention your cop, "He's one of the good ones."

I know you mean well.

Not long ago, my wife showed me an article in *Poets and Writers* (a trade magazine) titled, "I'm Writing to You," a collection of essays on race written by Black writers. The essay that caught her eye, "To My Precious Son" by Sharon Bell, was written as a letter (no wonder I liked it!), commenting on how the media drives the narrative of what a Black man is. There's the Athletic Black Man, Toxic Black Man, Cool Black Man, Charming Black Man, Thuggish Black Man and the list went on. Bell's premise was that the world sees Black men as caricatures defined and normalized by the media. "Isn't it similar for cops?" my wife asked me. "Everyone has an opinion about who cops are and what kind of person a cop is, and most people don't even know a cop."

She's right. More than anything else, the media is determining the narrative of who we are. Of course, there's the Racist Cop

— you see him everywhere — and Macho Cop, Control-Freak Cop, Authoritarian Cop, Donut-Eating Fat Cop, Dumb Hillbilly Cop, and just to balance things out, just to prove the media isn't biased, they often toss in "Officer Cuddles," who rescues cats from trees or takes the handicapped child for a ride in his squad car or does a cool break dance while directing traffic.

But who are cops really?

Why do you need to qualify — *But he's one of the good ones!* — when you mention what we do for a living?

Maybe because what you know, maybe all you know, is the media-created cartoons manufactured to make a story more interesting. What social justice crusaders rightfully campaign against — the stereotyping of groups — has been done to cops without protest on the nightly news almost every day for the past few years. The "racist cop" is systemic, the nation continues to be told.

And people believe it.

You believe it.

But it's not true.

Or fair.

No rational human being thinks it's okay to say young Black men all have the same temperament, background, attitudes, and beliefs.

Why is it okay to say this about cops?

Half a century ago, Patrick Murphy, police commissioner in New York City in the 1970s, tried to address this question by saying, more eloquently than I've been able to, that "for far too long [the public has] simply taken our police forces for granted or romanticized (or villainized) them beyond recognition in our television and movies; and this may be because some of us do not take cops seriously . . . but we need a better understanding of the role of the police in the context of our lives. Do we ask too much of the police or too little — or some of both? Do we ask them to simply be keepers of our gates or custodians of our morals? . . . Do we see them for what they are or what they should be — professionals providing a vital public service? Can we be satisfied to permit them to be just cops?"

Just cops. Jesus.

In other words, human beings.

Not stereotypes.

It's absurd that I have to remind people of this, even you — my friends, my wife's friends, some of our family. It angers me. It should be a given.

Does it matter that I've spent numerous afternoons on my own time mentoring elementary school kids in an after-school program consisting predominately of at-risk minority children? I helped them with math, worked with them on reading skills, served snacks, and played games. What about the nights I spent in a homeless shelter, again on my own time, so that men who were mostly Black would have a meal and a safe place to stay on bitter winter nights? The smell of dirty feet was overwhelming. I stayed awake, sitting in the dark at a minuscule desk with only the faint glow of small lamp to read by, and a symphony of snores, grunts, and farts as background music. Fifteen to twenty men of varying ages and problems, many of whom were mentally disturbed, alcoholic, drug-addicted, but in need of such simple things: sleep, safety, warmth.

I remember, too, receiving a call at home in the middle of the night from a distraught friend begging me to search for her son in the known drug haunts because he'd not come home and she was scared for him. I went in search of this child (a Black child) because I cared about his mother.

On another night, my corporal was called to check on the welfare of a young mom and her two children who were loitering in a hotel lobby. They had no place to go, no money. The infant was soiled and had no diapers and the other child was filthy, wearing tattered clothes. This corporal, with her own money, bought clothes and diapers for the children. The corporal was White; the children were Black. I mention this not because the race of those children mattered to her — or to me — but because it seems to matter so much to the media.

Again, I know you mean well, but I'm tired of hearing I'm the exception, or "we need more cops like you." I'm tired of you — my friends, my family — rushing to explain that no, no, you're not talking about me when you're talking about racist or bullying or power-hungry or fill-in-the-blank cops. God, no! You're talking about the cops in Minneapolis or Atlanta or Baltimore!

Maybe you believe this. Maybe I'd like to believe it. Why then do I feel I've got a stone in my gut? Maybe because you're jumping to conclusions, you're making assumptions, and when you start talking about systemic police racism, you are talking about me. It's insulting, but more than that, it hurts. It fucking hurts.

We don't need more cops like me.

There are already more cops like me.

There are about nine hundred thousand more cops like me, all across this country.

I wondered, what is it like to be a policeman, especially now, these days.
What is it like to be you?
— *Lucy by the Sea*, Elizabeth Strout

2

Letter to a Young Cop

There's so much I want to tell you, so much I want for you: to serve without injury and to end your career quietly, happily, and in good health after twenty, twenty-five — even forty — years with the knowledge that you've done your job well. I want for you to be filled with pride every day that you put on your uniform, your gun belt, your ballistic vest (always wear your vest, Young Cop). Mostly, I want you to feel both awe and humility at what an honor it is to be a police officer.

Young Cop, you will bear witness to people in the worst moments of their lives. Don't get bitter; don't become cynical. Instead, let your experiences make you more empathetic. Be grateful that circumstances haven't brought you to the same dark places you'll so often encounter others. You're going to see awful things in this career, things no one voluntarily chooses to witness, but you will also have the best seat in the house for this human pageant that we're all in.

More than three hundred years ago, in 1710, a constable from Boston by the name of Nicholas Boone published a book titled *The Constables Pocket-book: Or, A Dialogue Between an Old Constable and a New.* Written as a dialogue between an old and a young constable, the book was meant as a how-to manual to help new constables. I write to you with the same goal. Some of these letters will touch on subjects you learned in the academy, but most are about things that can't be taught. How you will come to define your role as a cop isn't, in the end, about tactics or law or government. It's about what you care about and value.

And what you don't.

In *The Constables Pocket-book*, the young constable asks the old constable, "I have taken the Oath, and hope to do my Duty, and therefore desire you to inform me, How I ought to manage this trust for the Publik good, and my own safety."

Managing this trust for the public good and my own safety. This is what I, an "old cop," want to convey to you, Young Cop.

And so, I write these letters. To you, mostly, but also to your family and friends; to your neighbors and to the communities you serve; to the people who love you and the people who fear you, and in their fear, may dislike you, perhaps even hate you. I write out of my own fear — and I've got plenty of it — but also out of my enormous hope that maybe these letters can be the beginning of some much-needed conversations: between old White cops like me and young Black men; between cops and the strangers whose lives we touch and change every day; between cops and their wives, cops and their kids, cops and other cops. I write to understand and I write to explain and I write because I believe we can all do better.

Because we have to.

*It had been a long process to get to that day — two years of background
checks, interviews, tests. An entire institution with a long history and a proud
tradition deciding I was worthy of wearing the badge.*
— *An Inconvenient Cop: My Fight to Change Policing in America,*
Edwin Raymond

3

Letter to a Young Cop About Becoming a Cop

Not long ago, I was driving somewhere with my wife, and I was pointing out the new neighborhood where one of my officers had just bought a home. I was happy for him, all the more so because I knew that after his divorce a few years back, he'd declared bankruptcy. Almost as an afterthought, I said, "Thank goodness that happened after he became a cop. He'd never have been hired if it had happened before."

My wife jerked her head up. "What do you mean? What do his financial problems have to do with his being a cop?"

"Everything!" I said. I was surprised she didn't understand this.

"No, not everything. Who cares if he had financial trouble? That's his business. He's a great cop, and a fantastic dad." (In my wife's eyes, being a good parent equals being a good person.)

She wasn't wrong about the officer. A man of few words, he mostly communicated with grunts, but kids worshipped him. He often babysat for other cops when they got into a child-care pinch. When his own kids were young, I'd see him in town with a gang of boisterous, unruly youngsters lollygagging behind him as he ran his off-duty errands. On duty, his calm under pressure was inspiring. He was the guy I'd want for backup. As an investigator, he had a bullshit meter that was so finely tuned criminals had no chance at playing him, so the ones who knew him answered his questions truthfully right from the get-go. This guy was a cop's cop.

But none of that would have mattered if, when he was being hired, he'd had money issues. "You're not looking at the big picture," I told my wife. "Someone who's having financial difficulties could be prone to bribery, blackmail, making unethical decisions. It shows a lack of responsibility. I'm not saying that's how he is. But that's how the admin looks at it, and when hiring, it's a concern. It has to be."

She grudgingly conceded that she hadn't considered this, but still, it didn't seem fair.

Maybe it isn't. But that's how it is.

I don't think the public has a clue what we go through to become cops, how many obstacles there are, and what kind of standards we have to meet. I remember how intimidated I was by the process. I was thirty-eight when I became a cop, and until that point, it was up to me how much of my life I wanted to share with anyone — even my spouse. But background investigators look at everything: If you played sports, were you a sore loser, overly aggressive, a glory hog? Or were you a team player? It matters. They'll ask your exes if you got jealous or were moody, why you broke up, and how you took the breakup. Even if you've been married for more than fifteen years, as one of my colleagues was when he became a cop, the investigators still tracked down his ex-girlfriends. He hadn't spoken to them in over a decade, but this didn't matter either. Those relationships are telling.

People laugh when I tell them a candidate for a police officer must have a past far more unblemished than that of a candidate for president. Yeah, right, they think, and roll their eyes. But just consider the last few presidents: Trump's behavior with women, Joe's foot-in-the-mouth gaffes and financial dealings, Obama's use of drugs, W. with his drinking problems, and Bill — Bill's list of transgressions is too long for this book.

I imagine a lot of people would be surprised, as my wife was, at how the most minuscule hiccups in a person's life — stuff most people wouldn't think twice about — money problems or a nasty break-up in high school, too many speeding tickets or a wild night in college, even one careless post on social media — can mean a police candidate is done.

Done.

It doesn't matter how physically fit she is, doesn't matter that she has the degree in criminal justice, doesn't matter that she's always dreamed of being a cop.

It.

Doesn't.

Matter.

A few years ago, I had on my shift a great seasonal officer (college students who work for our PD during the chaotic, tourist-slammed summers). This kid was a surfer with blond spikey hair who'd come from a police family — his uncle was a respected chief of police in a nearby town. This young man had always dreamed of being a cop. I used to tell him, "You're so enthusiastic you're getting on my damn nerves," but he was just eager and excited. He reminded me a little of myself. You know how it is when we start: We want to do it all, be great cops, be heroes, even though half the time we can barely figure out how to use the radio. I'm sure I drove my sergeant crazy, too.

When I learned this young man was returning for a second summer as a seasonal, I was glad he was assigned to my shift. I had a lot of hope for him. By then, he was close to being hired by another city's police department as a full-time officer. He was in the final stages of his background check. He couldn't wait to start the police academy that fall.

And then, in a conversation with his background investigator, he was asked if he'd ever been involved in any domestic problems. He mentioned that he and his dad had gotten into a heated argument a few months back and had been pushing and shoving each other. "It wasn't a big deal to us," he told the investigator. "But someone called the police." They came, realized it was nothing, filed a minor incident report, went on their way. The report was just protocol: All dispatched calls get assigned a complaint number, and a report is filed, documenting the police response even when it turns out to be nothing: a broken-down car, debris in the roadway, an argument called in by a third party that's over before the cops arrive. In the case of my seasonal officer, the report was labeled "domestic dispute with no crime." Again, for most people nothing would come of this beyond some embarrassment, maybe, the next time they ran into their neighbors, but whatever . . . It happens: Spouses argue, parents yell at their kids, siblings fight. No big deal.

Mentioning that incident to his background investigator, something my seasonal did willingly in an effort to be absolutely up-front about everything, resulted in his being fired from our department. Immediately. He couldn't even continue his summer job as a seasonal officer. And the city that had been close to hiring him? No longer interested. He was devastated. But no police department can afford to take a chance on a candidate with "domestic dispute" in his record. They just can't. No way.

Still, something that small — almost a non-incident — and his dream was derailed.

Being a police officer will affect every aspect of your life, Young Cop. It's not just a job. Everything — and I mean everything — is under scrutiny. I often tell my seasonal officers, "Beware, because once you've got that uniform on, although you may not realize it, everyone is watching you." But it goes so much deeper. It's not just about what you do when wearing the uniform; it's about how you live your whole life.

Even your choice of friends may impact your ability to be hired. How many other jobs can you say that about? My wife was outraged at this, too. I gave her the example of a guy whose best friend growing up started to go astray of the law, selling a little dope, maybe getting into some fights, going through a rough time. "No matter how long you've been friends," I told her, "even if he's a great guy, if you want to be a cop, you'd have to distance yourself."

"Are you serious?" she asked. "What about loyalty? What about not walking away when your friend is down?"

"You can be loyal," I told her. "But you can't pal around with the guy. It's not like old times, not if you want to be a cop. It shows a lack of judgment."

"How? If the person who wants to be a cop isn't doing any of the questionable things, what's the problem?"

"Well, think about it," I told her. "You're riding around with your pal one day; you're going to get a case of beer and have a barbecue. He gets stopped for a minor traffic violation and you don't realize it, but he's got a warrant out, which allows for a search, and before you know it, they've found a bag of narcotics under your seat — you can now get charged with possession and conspiracy to distribute. You're done if you want to be a cop. Finished."

My wife doesn't think this is fair either.

Maybe not. But it doesn't matter.

And it doesn't stop even after you become a cop.

How you behave in public, even off-duty, reflects on our profession. Losing your temper at your daughter's lacrosse game, screaming at the ref, not only makes you look bad as a parent, but as a police officer. Cops are supposed to keep their cool; they're not supposed to let little things get under their skin. If it's an accountant or an electrician or a lawyer screaming at the ref, no one is thinking, *jeez, that guy shouldn't be an accountant* or *I'd hate to have him as my electrician*, but they certainly will think, *man, that guy shouldn't be a policeman*.

People talk about police officers putting their life on the line, but what they rarely consider is how far that line stretches.

"What happens now?" (character asks a reporter after her Black
boyfriend is shot to death by a cop who thought the
boyfriend was assaulting a White woman).
*"It'll get investigated, the officer will be exonerated, and it'll be another
statistic in this country's long history of Black killings."*
"How can he be exonerated? He shot an unarmed man!"
— *Horse*, Geraldine Brooks

4

Letter to the Media About the Killing of Unarmed Suspects

The minute anyone hears that the police killed an unarmed suspect, it's easy to assume the killing was unjustified. Because, come on, a suspect who's unarmed? How can he pose a serious threat to an officer, especially when we carry such an arsenal of weapons?

He was unarmed! And they shot him! Unarmed!

You, the media, God, how quickly you grab hold of this word — unarmed — and you repeat it and repeat it and repeat it. It makes the story more tragic, more senseless, more emotional, and the rage it incites creates even more stories — of riots and calls for the officer to be dismissed, of police defunding. It's all about the story, isn't it? About making the story more.

And it works. That word *unarmed* becomes a battle cry. People say it with disdain and sadness and incredulity. How, how, could the police shoot another unarmed man? Good God, where will it end?

I want to believe that you who so blithely report the news are simply ignorant of what "unarmed" might mean. I want to believe that it's not about sensationalism, not about driving up your ratings. The story's so much more complicated, and I get it — you don't have time for complicated and soundbites don't work with complicated, but will you at least listen to my side, at least consider it the next time "unarmed" becomes the weapon you use against cops?

Not long ago, I stopped a car for a traffic violation and quickly suspected the young driver was intoxicated: glazed eyes, slurred speech, nonsensical answers to simple questions. Although the wide boulevard where I'd stopped him was mostly well-lit, this stretch of road was not; it ran south of the commercial district, giving way to well-manicured lawns and quiet streets. Large old trees and overgrown bushes made the road feel darker. I could still hear the low thrum of traffic on the main avenue a few blocks away where the bars were open, but it was nearing last call and the night was winding down. There might have been people strolling home, but I don't remember: I was focused on the suspect.

After I'd performed field sobriety tests and determined the man was seriously impaired, I told him he was under arrest and asked him to turn away from me and place his hands behind his back, so I could cuff him. Until that moment, he'd been cooperative, almost laid-back. Suddenly everything changed: His face tightened, he squinted, his lips got thin, and he adopted a fighting stance. He was clearly an athlete, strong and muscular, his movements fluid.

What I didn't know at the time was that this man, in addition to being drunk, abused steroids. It wouldn't take long before I discovered he also suffered from "roid rage" — extreme, often violent, mood changes (a symptom of steroid abuse). Later, I would also learn that he'd been a state champion wrestler and a successful MMA fighter.

Now, he shoved his hands into his pockets, ripped them inside out and slammed items to the ground: change, a small steel pipe, a lighter. His grace was gone. He was like a box truck trying to maneuver in a narrow alley. "Fuck you, asshole," he said. "I'm done!" and spun around to leave.

I grabbed his shirt by his shoulder, but he jerked away from me, raising his fisted hands, ready to attack. I quickly radioed: "24-A" (officer needs assistance), then pepper-sprayed him in the face with a strong burst.

It's a prerequisite that any officer carrying the spray has to be sprayed himself because it's both an aerosol and an intense inflammatory agent, which means chances are good the officer using it will be exposed. We need to know what it feels like and how to work through it. I'm also a pepper-spray instructor, so I have a lot of experience with its effects — which should start immediately: difficulty breathing; burning eyes, throat, and lungs; swelling lips and nose; hearing impairment and disorientation; sometimes all-out panic. Typically, it takes a good thirty minutes to start coming out of the effects.

That night, in the dim cone of light from a street lamp, I could see the heavy orange goo of the spray covering my suspect's face, but instead of all the reactions I'd seen in the past, he stared straight at me, shook his head from side to side, drool spraying from his lips, then made a deep guttural sound.

"I'm screwed," I said to myself.

The other full-time officer who had checked on me when I first radioed in that I was doing a DUI investigation was suffering with intestinal problems and had to leave. I'd told him I was okay because I thought I was. But I'd felt a premonition when he left, and maybe he did too, because he kept apologizing, saying, "Sorry, man; I'll be back as soon as I can."

Now that bad feeling was confirmed.

As the suspect came at me, he growled, "Why don't you just kill me? Better yet, why don't I just kill you?" And then he was grabbing me and grabbing the handle of my pistol, trying to wrench it from my holster. Thank God the holsters are designed so the pistol can only be removed a certain way.

Later, I would tell a friend it's a good thing cops can't know what's coming. We show up for work and it's an ordinary night until it isn't, until a man much stronger than we are wants to kill us.

I have no idea how long we struggled. It felt like a long time, but might only have been a few minutes. I couldn't free up my right hand to use my baton: I was afraid to let go of his hand, which was on the gun's handle. With my left arm, I kept trying to push him away, and I was yelling repeatedly, "Get back! Are you out of your mind? What's wrong with you? This is just a drunk driving charge!"

In the end, backup arrived, though it would take several officers to subdue him.

I was lucky.

Corporal Keith Heacook was not.

Corporal Heacook worked in a jurisdiction near mine. He was near my age and like me, he'd begun to think about retiring. He had a wife, a son.

At his funeral, his cousin, a retired police officer, spoke of how, as Corporal Heacook was getting ready to report for his midnight shift on the night that would mark his End of Watch, his thoughts were not about what was going to happen to him. They were, "does my kid have a game, do I got to go to the bank, did I get enough sleep for my side job . . . "

Little did Keith Heacook know that early on the morning of April 25, 2021, in a small town not far from the one where I work, he would be dispatched to a fight. It was 5 a.m., well into his shift. I imagine he was tired. *Two hours to go*, he was probably thinking, struggling to stay awake. Five a.m. seems like the darkest time of the night. The exhaustion slams into you, and the last thing you want to do is drink another coffee — you've been doing that all night, and all you want now, all you can focus on, is sleep. Two more hours. And then the call comes in, and it seems routine — they all do — and you don't mind because at least it will make the time go more quickly. The night he died, Corporal Heacook didn't have any more information about the suspect than I had when I stopped the guy who would wrestle me for my gun. This isn't uncommon.

Fight in progress. That's all he knew.

Corporal Heacook responded alone, without backup, because there was no backup.

He didn't know the attacker was hiding, waiting to surprise him, which he did.

The suspect knocked Keith Heacook out and repeatedly stomped on his head so severely that by the time officers arrived ten minutes later, Keith Heacook was brain dead.

The attacker was unarmed.

And the rest of the sad truth is this: Had Corporal Heacook fired his weapon and killed his assailant, you, the media, would have plastered it all over the news: another White cop killing an unarmed Black man.

Instead, Corporal Keith Heacook's story, his death, was barely a blip on the national news.

Why?

I don't understand; I'm not sure I can understand.

There's no monument to Corporal Heacook as there is to George Floyd. No poems being written by nationally known poets, poems that are winning awards, poems like the one my wife read this morning in *The New Yorker* commemorating Eric Garner.

Unarmed doesn't mean the officer was safe.

Unarmed doesn't mean the victim was innocent.

The story is more complicated — as stories usually are.

We yearn for the emergence of heroes, and it's demonstrative of their tremendous dignity that the first responders are always quick to repudiate this term, to deny its application: This isn't heroism, this is my job.
— "The Terms of Terror" in *American Audacity: In Defense of Literary Daring*, William Giraldi

5

Letter to a Young Cop on the Anniversary of 9/11

"I had this partner — Andrea," a friend of mine, a former NYC homicide detective told me not long ago. "We still call each other on 9/11. When the attack happened, I remember we were both staring out the window crying our eyes out. I saw a woman in a yellow skirt and a guy in a suit drop out of the sky, just quietly falling. I could swear his suit was pin-striped. I was four blocks away, I couldn't possibly see the pinstripes, but I felt like I could. They had jumped or fallen out of a window up in the World Trade Center. And okay, I don't know about the color of the guy's suit, but to this day, I remember the yellow skirt."

I was still a rookie that day, just two years into the job. Over two decades later, that day is still etched in my mind. God, the images of those people jumping from the heights of the buildings. And then, as if in slow motion, the towers crumbling down. Although I was hundreds of miles from the scene, I could feel the panic, and I choked on the dust. Nothing like this had ever occurred in our nation. And yet in that chaos and hysteria, who remained constant, controlled, and calm?

Exactly.

Cops.

Firefighters.

As the world raced from the horror, these men and women rushed toward it.

They always do, Young Cop. Jesus. They always do.

James Leahy was one of those officers. Last seen carrying oxygen tanks into the Towers. And his last words to his partner, captured on tape? *There are more people upstairs.* He was going to help them.

Officer John Perry, fluent in four languages and learning a fifth, was filing his retirement papers at the precinct that morning. He wanted to become a medical malpractice lawyer. But after hearing about the attacks, he ran several blocks to the World Trade Center. He was last seen running into the South Tower.

What about Captain Kathy Mazza, the first female commanding officer at the Port Authority Police Academy? She was last seen with Lieutenant Robert Cirri, carrying a woman down the steps when the North Tower collapsed.

Or Officer Kenneth Tietjen. As a kid, he was scared of two things: police cars and fire trucks. Apparently, his family never stopped teasing him about this.

And then there's Mark Ellis. Another of the seventy-one police officers who died running into those buildings. Only twenty-six years old, not much older, perhaps, than you. He'd always wanted to become a police officer, playing cops and robbers at age five with plastic handcuffs and a small notepad to write "speeding tickets."

Like all of us, he had big dreams and big plans.

And NYPD cop Ramon Suarez, who was closer to my age, left behind two daughters and a son. One of those daughters, Jillian, became a New York City police officer on October 15, 2018, seventeen years after her father died in the line of duty. Gillian is the name of my daughter, and I feel, especially today, connected to her father and to the other officers who gave their lives.

Don't ever forget those people, Young Cop.

You are now connected to them as well.

The PPD wasn't about arrests and statistics. It was about keeping the peace and doing right by people.
— Robert Parker's Colorblind, Reed Farrel Coleman.

6

Letter to the Friend Who Didn't Trust Me as a Cop

No doubt about it: Those officers who ran into the towers that day were heroes, and I know you agree that they should be remembered as such. I still love thinking about how the Halloween after that 9/11, a ton of little kids dressed up as cops and firemen, right there with all the other superheroes: Batman, Superman, the Flash, the Power Rangers.

You'd never guess that a lot of people still think of us as heroes if you watch mainstream media for half a second. Most of what you see there is the viral video (taken out of context) of some cop captured in the worst moment of his life when everything goes wrong and the world goes to shit. But day to day? People are grateful for what we do. You're one of them. You often thank me for my service.

So do a lot of average Joes, goofy kids being kids, gangly teens and moms with toddlers, guys working construction, young Black men — they stop me on the street all the time and thank me. Many of them engage me with questions about the job, or shake their heads and tell me, "I don't know how you do it." Strangers wish me the best and pray for my safety.

You have no idea how much I appreciate this, but I don't want to be mistaken as a hero.

I don't want that kind of baggage.

There are too many misperceptions and myths surrounding police work, and these myths not only isolate us, they alienate us from the very people who might need our help. Don't get me wrong: I love the myth of the stoic warrior cop as much as anyone. I picture someone like the Jesse Stone character in Robert B. Parker's detective novels. He'll do whatever he has to, even break the rules, if it brings down the bad guys and keeps his town safe. In the made-for-TV movies of these books, numerous scenes depict Stone, the police chief of a small town not so different from ours, sitting in the dark, nursing a Scotch, mourning his failed relationships, and staring into the sad eyes of his dog, the only creature who can truly understand him. Stone's a hero all right, though the job has taken a toll.

But here's the problem: Are we really heroes any more than the first-grade teacher who every day tries to teach kids who are too hungry to pay attention? More of a hero than my niece, a social worker in an inner-city Chicago prison where she works with juvenile gang members who don't want to be released because the minute they are, they'll probably get murdered? Are we more of a hero than the oncologist or the pediatric intensive care nurse? More of a hero than you, my friend, a woman in her seventies who devotes hours, days sometimes, driving hundreds of miles to help an ailing former colleague who has no one else to buy his groceries or take him to doctor appointments?

I don't think so.

The problem with being a hero starts with the definition: *a mythological or legendary figure often endowed with great strength or ability.*

Seriously? Are cops any of these things? Am I?

Mythological? Legendary?

Give me a break.

What I especially resist is this idea of the hero as special, extraordinary, not like everyone else. That's the last thing we need. Hasn't this charge brought us as much condemnation — cops think they're above the law — as it has accolades?

And it's not true.

Clearly, I can't speak for all cops, but I'm just a regular guy who goes to work and does his best, not because I have a burning desire to save the world or even to make it a better place, though I hope I do. I show up because I have a family to support, a mortgage, and until a year ago, a mother with dementia to care for. But honestly? One of the biggest motivations? I've got a motorcycle I love riding, which means solitary week-long motorcycle trips that need funding.

In other words, I have a whole life outside of work. I love to surf, and I've been so consumed by it that even in the winter I can go out in thirty-five-degree water to charge nor'easter swells, looking for that perfect ride, grabbing for the rush and adrenaline only a large winter wave can give. I care for my Harley like it's another kid, and I belong to a traditional three-patch motorcycle club. I paid my dues and worked hard as a prospect to earn the trust of my brothers in the club. These men mean the world to me. They, too, are regular guys who have families and work hard in their chosen professions. We do a ton of charity work and I'm proud of that as well. At home, I love trying out new recipes, the spicier and more exotic the better. I read thrillers — everything by Deon Meyer, John Sandford, Robert Crais, Ace Atkins, and Lisa Gardner, though damn, I wish her mysteries didn't all have to involve children. It's brutal. I'm probably addicted to the same TV shows everyone's addicted to, and I love Hallmark Christmas movies, the sappier the better.

Yeah, I'm a cop and I'm proud — I am so proud — of my career, but my interests and my life are so much bigger, so much more.

Which means I go to my job for the same reason my surfing buddy Kent goes to his job as an electrician. (And why is no one calling him a hero, thanking him for his service?) He too works in extreme temperatures, deals with emergencies, helps those in need. If the power goes out, even in the middle of the night, he's there. He's a good guy — as I am, but I do what I do because I signed on to do it. That's all. It's what I chose.

In a way, Kent's lucky no one's calling him a hero. Because once you've been placed on that pedestal, you're not allowed any imperfections, not allowed to fail, not allowed to be human.

People forget this. My own family forgets, and you, my good friend, have forgotten. Even I sometimes do. It's heady stuff to be a hero.

It's also lonely.

Years ago, Kent commented to me, "You're a cop. You don't get afraid." I was stunned. Kent's a brilliant businessman, and we've been friends for decades. He's watched my kids grow up, was the only person I confided in when I was getting divorced, is the guy I call for financial advice. He introduced me to the woman who's now my wife.

And yet.

He thought I wasn't afraid because I'm a cop?

"You're out of your mind," I told him. "Everyone gets scared; cops just have to face their fears."

But I still think about this, the belief that we aren't as afraid as everyone else — or maybe that we're not supposed to be.

It bothers me.

To not be afraid is to not be human.

I've got plenty of fears. I'm terrified of flying. And sure, I know that sounds cliché, but I get nauseous, have trouble breathing, especially during takeoff and landing. My son is twenty-five, and every Friday and Saturday night when he's out with friends, I can't help but feel dread at the thought that he'll be maimed or killed in a drunk-fueled traffic accident. I've seen it too many times. The same is true for my twenty-eight-year-old daughter who thinks nothing of jumping on a plane by herself, going to strange cities for ballet auditions. She hasn't witnessed the evil that I have, and so I worry she may be careless. Again, a sense of dread consumes me when she's gone. My father spent years in hospice clinging to life, and I spent years afraid every time my phone rang that it was the final call from his wife. That call finally came; I felt like a boy at the thought that my father was gone.

Yes, I feel fear. I'm human.

The other myth about cops, and it's just as dangerous, is the one about the racist cop, the corrupt cop, the power-hungry cop who lords his authority over others. And hell, forget myth. Ever since George Floyd was murdered — and he was, no doubt — people just assume that "these truths are self-evident." It reminds me of the old adage, "If you tell a lie enough times, it no longer appears to be a lie." In every profession there are practitioners who absolutely suck at their jobs, but the only profession I see getting an across-the-board condemnation for the poor performance of a tiny few is the police. Hell, politicians get a much greater pass than cops and that's saying something.

Again, I'm not saying lousy cops don't exist, but they're not the majority, not even close. Research in criminal justice finds that individuals choose a career in law enforcement for two key reasons: to help others and for job security. And wielding power over others? That's not substantiated by research either. It's not something most cops want or enjoy. Still, the belief persists for the same reason the belief in hero cops persists: It makes a good story.

I was confronted with this bad-cop myth recently by you, someone I love and have always had a rapport with. You couldn't be more to the left of the political spectrum and I'm pretty far to the right, but we just connected from the moment we started talking. I love this about us, and I cherish our friendship. I still do. But not long ago, you found the wallet of a man you believed to be an illegal immigrant and you asked me what you should do.

"Just bring it to the station," I said. "I'll take care of it."

"What? I can't do that!" you replied. You wanted to help the guy, you explained, not get him arrested. Wasn't it my job to report him to immigration?

"That's not my job at all," I assured you. "We return found property (wallets, phones, licenses) to owners all the time, no matter who they are."

But you never brought the wallet in.

In that situation, I wasn't your friend; I was a cop, not to be trusted.

That really stung, but I get it. You come from a satellite world far away from mine and have almost zero contact with cops. You only know what you see on the news.

I know — I really do — that your distrust of cops wasn't really about me.

And yet, of course, it was.

African Americans are stopped 20 percent more than White drivers according to the Stanford Police Project.
— "Breathing While Black," Yanick Rice Lamb, in *We Refuse to Be Silent: Women's Voices on Justice for Black Men*, ed. Angela P. Dodson

7

Letter to the Young Black Motorist

A summer night at the height of my town's tourist season. It's after midnight, and the bar crowd is thinning out. Until around ten, the restaurants are still serving, which means the arcades and kitschy T-shirt shops are crowded as well. The sidewalks are thronged with families, groups of friends, and clusters of women on their "girls' night out." But by midnight, the town is almost quiet, the sidewalk empty but for an occasional drunk stumbling home or exhausted-looking parents pushing sleeping toddlers in strollers and carrying worn-out kids slumped over their shoulders. Employees from the pizza and ice cream shops are hauling out garbage and hosing down the sidewalks.

I'm parked on the main avenue, the only street most tourists know to get in and out of town. At this time of night, the street is poorly lit — there's a closed realtors office, an insurance company, a darkened Starbucks. Drivers can't see my patrol car from a distance. I can't see the actual drivers either, but if they're intoxicated, it's easy to spot the driving traits of a drunk: speeding, lane drifting, hitting the brakes every other second, or sometimes being overly cautious, crawling at fifteen miles per hour when the speed limit's twenty-five.

I'm five hours into my shift, hoping the night stays calm. And that's when you drive by in your older-model Jeep with no taillights. Of course, I pull you over. This isn't a cheesy stop — pulling over someone for a stupid little infraction that causes no harm, like a broken side-mirror or faulty muffler. No taillights at night — that's potentially dangerous.

As I get out of my car, I notice your license plate is expired.

I approach you, the driver, a young Black man, and ask for your license, car registration, and proof of insurance. You tell me you don't have your license; it has been suspended. Then you say, "Here we go: another example of the police keeping the Black man down."

Wait. What? I stopped you because your taillights were out, and it's night. End of story. But I get it: You and I might be strangers, but an awful history stretches between us. I think about it for a second, take a breath, then say, "Hey, man, jump in my car."

"Why?" you say. Fear darts across your face, and I understand that too.

"Humor me; you're not under arrest. Jump in the front seat, not the back. I want to show you something." I'm asking you to trust me, and it's a big ask: You have reason not to.

But you get in and I drive to where I was parked. As cars pass by, I ask, "What color is that driver? Can you tell if it's a man or a woman?"

"I can't tell," you say.

I glance at you. "Exactly."

"Ah, man."

That was it. I watched you drive off. I have no idea what you thought of that encounter, if you thought of it at all.

I'm not suggesting "Driving While Black" isn't an issue, only that on the night we crossed paths, it wasn't.

Ponder long and hard upon this point: the mere decision to be a surgeon
[or a cop] will not magically confer upon you the dexterity,
compassion, and calmness to do it.
— *Letters to a Young Doctor*, Richard Selzer

8

Letter to the Young Cop Who Should Not Be a Cop

Last night, driving home from dinner with friends, in a good mood, laughing and debriefing about the night — which is always the best part of any outing — my wife and I were stopped by you. You said my wife hadn't used her turn signal when changing lanes. It was late, the highway empty, and the stop seemed "cheesy." You were probably hunting for a DUI, looking for any violation to stop a car. That's fine. I get it. Enforcing impaired driving laws isn't what most people think. Usually, cops don't see the drunk driver drifting back and forth across lanes, clipping the mirrors of parked cars, or driving the wrong way with his headlights off. Most drunk drivers, even very drunk drivers, can hold their shit together when they see a cop, so success in this kind of enforcement is all about finding ways to make the traffic stop: the headlights aren't on, the driver fails to use her turn signal, a taillight's out. Once we've made the stop and we're talking to the driver, we can see the signs: the glassy eyes, the slurred speech. And if the signs aren't there, fine; you wish the driver a good night and send her on her way. No harm done. After all, the goal is to stop drunk drivers before they lose that short-term focus and hit someone — or worse. So, the more stops a cop makes when she's doing DUI enforcement, the more likely that she'll get that drunk off the road. It's an inconvenience, but it saves lives.

That said, I know my wife used her turn signal; I remembered the *click, click*.

My wife was respectful to you, and I identified myself as a cop, so you let her go with a warning. All good. Until a few minutes later when you pulled us over again, and now you were aggressive, berating my wife for still not using her signal. "Twice!" you shouted. "I watched you!"

But again, I'd watched my wife use the signal. And so, nicely, I said to you, "Maybe the bulb burned out. We'll get it replaced as soon as possible." Not a big deal, except you never considered there might be a reasonable explanation for the lack of a signal. You automatically assumed we were disrespecting you, and you became consumed with the need to assert your authority. I find this troublesome. What if I, a fellow officer, hadn't been in the car? I don't like the way you spoke to my wife. It's not the way to speak to anyone, and it made me question if you're the kind of man I want to see in our profession.

The answer is no.

You are part of the problem.

"As a cop, don't you get that way?"
"What way?"
"Cynical, I guess . . . . Don't you ever get to the point where you
expect the worst from people all the time?"
—*The Storied Life of A. J. Fikry*, Gabrielle Zevin

9

Letter to the Cop Who Never Imagined He'd Become a Cop

It never crossed my mind to become a cop either. I liked cop shows, but being a police officer? No fucking way. I was an artist, and I had big dreams. I was going to be a great sculptor; my name would go down in history.

So, patrol officer?

Sergeant in some small town no one's ever heard of?

No.

Being a cop wasn't something I ever aspired to. Wasn't something anyone I knew ever aspired to.

It makes me laugh to read of how the Cincinnati Police, one of the first to establish both a "gymnasium" and a "School of Instruction" for its officers in 1887 and 1888, described their ideal officers like this: *A model Cincinnati Police officer must . . . be a perfect specimen of physical manhood, able to pass a physical examination more exacting than that required of the West Point Cadet, [be] as symmetrical as an Apollo, as strong as a Hercules, as enduring as iron.*

As symmetrical as Apollo?

Seriously?

As enduring than iron?

Cincinnati wasn't the only city with lofty ideals for its police. In 1887, NYPD Chief of Police George Walling went further: *Let us imagine an institution in which the guardian of the peace can learn to make a pleasant bow, to walk with grace, to shake hands with dignity, to lift his hat in a courtly way, or to extend his protecting arm to a lady with Chesterfieldian decorum.*

Chesterfieldian decorum? Give me a break.

It was absurd then — and still is — to think police departments could attract that kind of man, that kind of talent, that kind of class, eloquence, sophistication, you name it, and continue to offer salaries that were among the lowest in local government service. And sure, although salaries and benefits have become better in a lot of jurisdictions, it's too often the case that the communities with the most crime and the most need for great cops are also the communities least able to afford it.

Believe it or not, it was the Great Depression that initially improved the quality of applicants to our field. Men who before the 1929 crash would never have considered joining the force did so in the 1930s out of economic necessity. The NYPD class of 1940 not only contained college graduates, but numerous lawyers and CPAs.

I like this piece of history because this is why I became a cop: I needed a steady job. With benefits. I'm betting you became a cop for similar reasons. Of course, we're not supposed to admit this. We're supposed to have dreamed of being cops our whole lives! We want to make the world a better place, save lives, etc., etc. And okay, fine, maybe we do. But it started for me with needing a paycheck and medical insurance and wanting to pay my mortgage.

By the time I made the decision to carry the badge, I'd been an artist for over a decade. I'd gone through years of apprenticeships in the skills required to make sculpture. That was my passion. Picture it: me in a black porkpie hat, long hair, wearing denim coveralls and a leather welding jacket. I'd spend twelve, fourteen, hours in the foundry, the glitter of silica dust in the air, old-school hip-hop music blaring over the noise of the machines as I worked on my latest project. As a sideline I spent almost a year in Europe and learned the art of decorative blacksmithing. I wasn't just some wannabe artist dressing in funky clothes and talking about art without ever putting in the time. I was the guy who was actually building the sculptures that major artists like Seward Johnson or Isaac Witkin or Joel Shapiro were creating. I loved this life. It was fun and exciting, but it was also hard, dirty work and physically demanding. And Jesus, the pay was low, generally just above subsistence.

By the time I became a husband and father, I was working all the time to make ends meet, and it was exhausting. I had a metal shop, a business, and I did commissions, creating decorative iron gates and elaborate railings for well-heeled estates, but it wasn't enough. I knew something had to change. I'd just finished a major bronze commission for the University of Maryland, and I felt I'd made my mark. I could leave sculpture without any regrets — and I did. Never looked back. Oddly, just after retiring from full-time policing, I was invited back to the University of Maryland to give a speech at the twenty-five-year rededication of my sculpture. What struck me was how permanent my bronze is and how quickly my life has passed.

The winter I first considered becoming a cop, I was supplementing my income by working long hours as a commercial fisherman. I'd head out to the boat by three a.m. in the freezing cold. By law we couldn't start fishing until sunrise, but it would take a good hour to motor the forty-foot vessel the sixteen miles into the ocean. It would be dark, a faint line of light coming up at the horizon. Winter seas are rough with large swells and gusting winds, and we'd be out there until sunset, pulling steel dredges the size of small cars across the bottom of the sea to rake up clams, crabs, and conchs. We'd head to shore once the sun set, but there was still the frigid and seemingly interminable journey back to dock, the cleaning of the boat, the selling of the day's catch. These were long brutal days, and while the work was profitable, it was also dangerous. I had no health insurance, and if something were to happen to me, my wife and daughter would have nothing.

Still, it never occurred to me to become a police officer — not once — until one night, exhausted after a day on the water, I heard on the local news an interview with the chief of police from a nearby town. He spoke about the arduous process of becoming a cop, of how difficult it was to get and retain good officers, and I thought, *I can do that.*

Three months later, I was hired by the chief I'd seen on TV.

I guess I'm writing to reassure you. One of the best cops I ever worked with was a plumber first; another, who didn't become a cop until he was in his forties, was a medical salesman. It's fine if being a cop wasn't your calling.

What matters is that it is now.

The fatal funnel was the way they taught you [at the police academy]
how easy it was to go from a safe place to a place
where you've lined yourself up for something bad to happen . . .
— The Best Minds, Jonathan Rosen

10

Letter to My TAC Officers at the Police Academy (Teach, Advise, Counsel)

I was thirty-eight years old when I entered the Delaware State Police Academy. Suddenly, I was living in a barracks, sleeping in a huge open squad bay with nearly forty other men, most of them almost half my age. I was away from my wife and daughter. I was sleep-deprived — it wasn't unusual for one of you to wake us in the middle of the night and take us out for a run wearing flip-flops as running shoes. I was a husband and a father, I'd owned a business for many years, had worked construction and been a commercial fisherman, and now I was reduced to a nothing-recruit, screamed at by you, spittle flying in my face for some minor infraction. It could be anything; it was anything: a thread dangling on my uniform, a forgotten radio ten-code, a spattering of the water in the sink after using it, a fucking dust bunny under my bunk.

Our days began when it was barely light. At least a three-mile run, a shower, then someone would yell "Attention," and we'd snap into line, shoulders back, eyes forward, as you inspected us: bunks properly made, shoes polished, uniforms crisp. Afterward, I and three other recruits reported for flag-raising detail, a precise and solemn ceremony that started the day. After breakfast (which, however nourishing, lacked desperately needed coffee), we headed to the classroom until lunch.

In those first three months, during our supposed "break time" between classes, you would order us to the "dog patch," where the canine units were run, and in this parched dirty field adjacent to a parking lot, you'd order us, in the heat of the day, to do an assortment of calisthenics. Sweaty, filthy, reeking of dog shit, you'd then discipline us because our uniforms were dirty!

I hated being at the police academy, hated the way you treated us, even though I understood the reason for it. As police officers, we're often sleep-deprived, running on fumes nine or ten hours into a twelve-hour shift, but still, in a matter of minutes, even seconds, we've got to make life-altering decisions. As officers, too, we can never lose our cool. You were preparing us for this, for all the times some drunk cuffed to the bench in the station would tell us over and over — and over! — how little our dicks were or what he planned to do with our wives or girlfriends. And it wouldn't only be those assholes we had to deal with, but regular citizens who, when we stopped them for speeding, would remind us of what losers we were to be spending time harassing them when there was real crime to attend to. We'd be able to just smile, nod, and remain polite because of what you taught us.

Afternoons in the academy, it was back to the classroom until early evening, the lowering of the flag, then another run, some as long as twelve miles, some through swampy mud or freezing rain. It felt unrelenting. But you were right there with us, leading the run.

Monday, boxing day, was the exception to this routine. Boxing's crucial. "You become a cop, you're going be assaulted at some point," you told us. "So, you better learn to fight." It's true. I didn't know it then, but I would never, in twenty-five years, fire my gun at another human being (I'd have to shoot wounded or sick animals). I'd use my taser only twice, my pepper spray a handful of times. I never struck anyone with my baton.

But I would defend myself many times with my hands and fists.

Thursday nights were even more special: We cleaned the entire academy. You remember, don't you? How afterward, while you did a thorough inspection, you had us lie in the dead cockroach position (on our backs, arms and legs in the air). It was excruciating. After dinner, more courses, often dealing with nighttime patrol procedures. And then more chores, always more chores.

In our daytime classes, you taught us traffic and criminal procedure, report writing, ticket and warrant writing, Delaware State Law, constitutional law, use-of-force guidelines, and more. The course on search warrants involved using a nearby hotel, where you had us role-play high-risk warrants: knock and enter, move quickly before evidence could be destroyed. These are among the most dangerous acts police engage in. We spent a week at the firing range; another week at the Department of Motor Vehicles, practicing tactical driving skills; another week at the Delaware Criminal Justice Information Systems Training Center, learning to use the computer programs involved in accessing information, filing reports, and creating warrants. No matter what we were doing, though, you were there between classes or as we lined up for meals, getting in our faces, asking questions, making us do squats and push-ups right there in the hallways if, God forbid, we weren't quick enough, loud enough, or forgot the damn answers.

This was our life Monday through Friday for six months. I watched the seasons change from the squad bay windows, where I would stare out at the highway and fantasize about hitchhiking home (we had to surrender our car keys to you on Monday mornings). In our class of about forty men and ten women, we lost fifteen recruits who either quit or were let go. It never occurred to me to quit, though I longed for Friday nights when I could get in the car, stop at the gas station down the road that had a Dunkin' Donuts, get the tallest coffee they had and an old-fashioned doughnut (though I don't even like doughnuts). When I arrived home an hour away, my then two-year-old daughter Gillian would be waiting for me on the front steps in her best party dress.

Monday morning I left my home in the darkness to get back for inspection at 7 a.m. As soon as I saw the headquarters radio towers, the knot in my stomach that would last all week began to form.

All of this was just getting us ready to be put on the street with other cops so that we could begin learning what it really meant to be a cop. Most agencies require another nine weeks of field training after we leave you. We're on duty with a seasoned officer who watches as we make our first traffic stop, go to our first domestic call, handle our first DUI. They analyze our driving, our safety techniques, study how we interact on calls, how we perform under stress — the list is endless.

And then it's our first night on duty alone and things happen, and we figure them out. And then it's our second month, and then we've been at it for a year. At some point we arrive at a call and instead of worrying about what we're going to do, we show up knowing that whatever it is, all those classes in the academy, all those early morning runs, all the nights away from our family, all the practice scenarios so that no matter what we were doing (even just approaching a car) we did it safely, all the times you pointed out our failings, screamed, yelled at us to run faster, do twenty more push-ups — all of those times trained us for this moment. Somewhere along the line, all those lessons became second nature.

We joked endlessly at the academy that the acronym TAC — Teach, Advise, Counsel — was bullshit. It should have been Torture, Abuse, and Command, but in the end, Teach, Advise, Counsel is what you actually did.

Thank you.

Being a policeman is . . . I like my place. I like my life. I want to keep both.
— *We Begin at the End*, Chris Whitaker

11

Letter to the Officer Who Showed Me the Ropes My First Night on Duty

I think of you every time Christmas rolls around, which is why I'm thinking of you now. The town where I work, not so far from the town where you and I once patrolled together, is getting ready for the holidays. City workers wrap garland around lampposts, hang twinkle lights in the branches of the Bradford pears lining the main avenue. The Friday after Thanksgiving we'll have a big tree-lighting ceremony at the bandstand, and the first Tuesday in December, we'll have an old-fashioned holiday parade.

It reminds me of that first Christmas.

Do you remember?

It was actually my first night on duty after graduating from the academy. Midnight to eight a.m. I was thirty-nine years old, my daughter was two and a half, my wife four months pregnant with my son.

You were showing me the ropes that night. You, too, were a dad, with three-year-old triplets at home. I'd met your wife, and all these years later, I can still picture her — a tiny woman, pretty, whom I'd met when the department introduced me to the town council.

Around two a.m., we drove to your home on the outskirts of town, where your children and wife were asleep. The house was dark but for the glow of the Christmas lights. Silently, we pulled wrapped presents from closets and other hiding places and arranged them under the tree. You knew you might not get home in time to see your children as they raced downstairs in the morning to see what Santa had brought.

I was on duty a lot of Christmases — all cops are. How many holidays did I stagger bleary-eyed into my living room after working the night shift, my kids awaiting my arrival before beginning their Christmas savagery? I was always so thankful for their patience, especially because more than once I fell asleep sitting on the couch in my uniform, watching the Christmas morning madness unfold.

But other times, I simply missed — I know you did too — our kids' birthdays, wedding anniversaries, Thanksgivings. I've never been able to celebrate the Fourth of July, a mandatory work day in my beach resort, where the fireworks over the ocean draw such enormous crowds that traffic is blocked for hours after the display. I missed the party to celebrate my father's election to the city council, and I missed the literary reading my favorite aunt gave shortly before she unexpectedly died. I say this without complaint, though not without regret. It's part of our job. We miss special times with our families, so others will have those times with theirs.

I'm not sure how much people really think about this, and I wish they did.

Any time a person's in trouble, he can call 9-1-1 and expect that we'll respond. It's been this way since 1833 when Philadelphia became the first US city to employ both day and night watchmen, thus beginning the trend that still defines policing nearly two hundred years later.

Right now, even if it's three a.m., somewhere nearby, a cop is on duty. Maybe it's you. I know you moved on to the state police after a long hiatus from being a cop at all.

The last time I worked on Christmas Eve, I dropped by the Catholic church for midnight mass. I slipped in through the huge oak doors, trying to stand unobtrusively just inside, ready to leave if a call came in. The place was full, and it felt warm with all the bodies packed together. I loved seeing the Christmas outfits: holly-patterned sweaters; Santa Claus and reindeer ties; little girls in velvet dresses and lace tights; women in red wool coats. My own kids were grown (as are your triplets), and I missed them, their younger, trusting, believing-in-Santa selves.

It's a strange feeling to be standing in a church in a police uniform, ballistic vest and gun belt. I was only an observer, not really a participant. I couldn't be. And then my radio blasted, and I was gone — to deal with whatever problem had come in. If I did my job well, no one would have even realized I'd disappeared. By the time the service was over, by the time families were headed out to their cars, perhaps snow was beginning to fall, and they'd forgotten all about the cop in the back of the church.

But I've never forgotten you, Charlie. I think of us tucking presents under the Christmas tree my first night on duty, and I feel — have always felt — grateful to have been a part of that small task. It wasn't long after that your wife was killed in a car accident. In a way, our being "elves" that night allowed you to still be part of your family's last Christmas together. Of all the things you showed me about how to be a cop, this was the most important.

Joe: Mom, could I ever be a policeman?
Jane: Perhaps, darling, if you're good.
Joe: Are all policeman good?
Jane: Yes, dear, as good as gold.
— *Cavalcade*, Act I; Scene VII, Noel Coward

12

Thank-You Letter to My Seasonal Officers

One of the best things about my police department, and what makes it unique, is you, our seasonal officers. November to May, the department runs pretty smoothly with our seventeen full-time officers. Sure, during the cooler months we have jumping nights — Halloween, St. Patty's Day, and no shit, any time there's a full moon — but we're never overwhelmed.

When the weather turns warm, though, watch out. The floodgates open. We go from a fight to a domestic assault to another fight to a traffic accident to a possible burglary, a missing child, a drunk driver, *fuck!* another damn fight and when will it end? It's hard to breathe, hard to keep our heads in the game as we boomerang from one thing to the next to the next. Our quaint little town of twelve hundred isn't so quaint or so little anymore. Plenty of weekends we'll have as many as sixty thousand people all crammed into an area not much bigger than one square mile. So, no way: two or three officers per shift can't handle the chaos.

Seas-ass-onals, I call you on the days you try my every last nerve.

Until this year, you had to be at least nineteen years old to be a seasonal. That's young. Too young, and it scares the crap out of me.

Not old enough to drink but you're going to arrest people? And now, because so few people want to be a cop anymore, or their parents are scared out of their minds to even think of their child becoming a police officer, we had to lower that age to eighteen just to get the minimal amount of help.

You attend a six-weekend training academy in basic criminal and traffic law, laws of arrest, search and seizure, etc. There's no way a weekend academy can prepare you to be dropped onto the street to patrol. It's my job to make sure you go home safe, and my job to turn you into useful "tools," which means I need you to be my eyes and ears on the street. Still, you have full arrest powers — and you need to. Although you're prohibited from responding to major crimes in progress (robberies, burglaries, domestic assaults), you're sent to fights, drunk-and-disorderlies, thefts, and drug offenses. Without your help, many — hell, probably most — of the minor crimes such as shoplifting, drinking booze on the beach, and that kind of thing would be ignored. There's no way the full-time officers can deal with it. But more than that, I've been in a tight spot with some amped-up dirtbag criminal who sure as hell wasn't going to listen to anything I had to say and was looking for a fight, and let me tell you, nothing made me happier than to see a couple of young, fit, overly zealous, pumped-on-adrenaline seasonals show up.

I still see you guys in my head: Keats and Henry, Joe, Brian, Chloe, and Kate — you're all full-time cops now.

Still, when I think of a typical seasonal officer, the picture that comes to mind is the young woman from a few years back who came from a small farm in a no-one-has-heard-of-it rural town. Her father drove her here. He was worried. It was the first time she'd rented her own apartment, always living in the dorms or at home. She had a face people trust, maybe a little too round but pretty, and Dad feared predators would sense her vulnerability. She was a dreamer. She wanted to help people, wanted to make a difference.

She wanted to be a cop.

Dad wasn't so sure how he felt about his daughter's career.

And this was before George Floyd, before all the defund-the-police rallies.

As a parent myself, I empathized with that dad and I empathize now with your parents. But because I'm intimately aware of what this job entails, because I understand its dangers as well as its joys — and don't let anyone tell you there isn't plenty of joy to be found in this job — and because I know the Hollywood portrayal of our profession is far from the reality, I would be proud if my son or daughter chose this career. Of course, I'd worry. That's the job of every parent. But this is an honorable, even a noble profession, and I admire you for giving it a try. I want your parents, friends, grandparents, and anyone else wringing their hands and asking, "are you sure . . . " to encourage and support you. I want them to believe in you and, more than that, I want them to believe you're going to make this world a better place to live in.

Because you are.

Part of what you bring to the game is your astonishment at things I now regard as routine. You're stunned, for example, to encounter adults your parents' ages — even your grandparents' ages! — acting in a degrading manner. And your shock, naivete, disbelief — you have no idea how much I wish I still had this. I don't, and it bugs me. I lost my capacity for surprise long ago, and that's a sad thing to say. When I have an obnoxious sixty-something-year-old woman so drunk that she bites — bites! — a stranger in a bar, and then, when the EMT is trying to get her into an ambulance to take her to detox, she kicks the EMT and urinates all over herself (and me), I'm mad, I'm irritated — it's fucking disgusting — but I'm not surprised. I'm not even fazed. And shouldn't I be?

Yes.

Jesus, yes!

You guys remind me that what I see day in day out, is not the norm. And your astonishment — *How can someone that age act like this? How does this happen to a person?* — reminds me to be curious.

I've lost this too.

Wonder, astonishment, curiosity: Are there any more important qualities? And yet, if you're going to succeed in this career, you've got to tamp those qualities down for your own survival.

As cops, we're taught to protect ourselves physically. It's what we try to train you to do in those measly six weeks before we put you on the street. Later, if you decide to stay with this career, you'll be trained in a hundred other things that will hopefully keep you and others physically safe. But where's the training for any of us in how to protect our emotions? How do you remain compassionate without becoming vulnerable to harm? How do you hold onto the curiosity and wonder you have at twenty-one — or hell, eighteen! — while staying hypervigilant to danger? Is it even possible?

I want it to be.

This is the kind of thing I think about during those crazy summer months when the bars have finally closed, and the town is quiet, and I walk the boardwalk with you, my seas-ass-onals. I ask you, "Can you really see yourself doing this for a career?" and "Why do you want to?"

These walks give me great joy even though we don't have much time — there's always paperwork and after twelve hours on duty, we all just want to go home. And then, before I know it, summer ends, you're returning to school, the weather grows colder, the days shorter. I might not hear from you or about you until a year or two later, when I get a call: Another police agency wants to hire you; can I talk to the officer doing the background check?

I love these calls. As I sift through my memories, evaluations, and records, I'd like to believe that maybe something that happened on my shift or something I said on some sweltering night as you and I walked the boardwalk together, pausing to remind some guy smoking a cigarette that it's not allowed, might have helped you to make the decision to do this job for a living.

Often we forget that the supposedly anonymous are the ones who form the true glue of the world.
— *American Mother*, Colum McCann with Diane Foley

13

Letter to the Admin Who Doesn't Have a Clue What Community Policing Really Is

It's your latest feel-good phrase: community policing. You and your politician pals can't get enough of it. Yes, yes, we need more community policing! Community policing is the answer! Cops just need to get out of their cars, stroll the streets, chat with the people in their neighborhoods.

And yeah, of course it's a good idea. Is there anyone who doesn't agree? It's easy, safe, a win-win! No wonder you love the phrase.

I think of how, every summer, the international students show up in our town to work for the summer. They're from all over — Turkey, Eastern Europe, Ireland, Uzbekistan, Egypt. Our department reaches out to the newcomers, instructing them in things like bike safety because this is their main mode of transportation. The department also attends some of the potluck dinners a local church has for them. You're always at those events, Chief, and if not you, one of your lieutenants. Big smiles, shaking hands with the students, maybe taking a group photo. The public information officer posts it on the department's Facebook page or sends it out with a quick press release. A day or two later one of the patrol cops might pull the photo up on his phone and show everyone in the locker room before shift change. We laugh, crack jokes. "Does the admin really think this is what community policing is?" someone might ask.

"The admin wouldn't know community policing if it hit them in the ass," someone else will joke.

Because those photo ops have nothing to do with what real community policing's about. And for the record? Community policing isn't new either.

Community policing is where policing started, and for good cops, it's not a buzzword or a program or an initiative. It doesn't have "three key elements," or "four strategic components" that can be illustrated through colorful graphics or on a flow chart. Google "community policing" and that's what you find: glossy brochures and PDFs that are pages long. It irritates me to no end. Because these graphs and documents and brochures are just so many words, and community policing is exponentially simpler and exponentially more complex. It's like air: absolutely necessary and always there — even if most people never think about it.

What community policing is not is your Wednesday afternoon "Coffee with a Cop" gathering at the library where you, a nonpatrol police administrator, joke, laugh, yuk it up, and answer questions from attendees who have the time and luxury to attend this midday, midweek meeting. Those attendees are probably not the ones who actually need community policing. Not the homeless, not the addicts, not the kids living in the Section 8 apartments just outside of town. These meetings are just one more feel-good photo op, and there's no harm in them, but like your slick brochures and PowerPoint presentations, they have nothing to do with community policing, which is often unpaid, unending, grueling, and mostly a thankless undertaking typically done by patrol officers.

Community policing is when a street cop takes time whenever he's on duty to check on a disabled manic Vietnam vet who speaks in imagery, jumping from one picture in his head to the next, without any of the usual connections that allow the listener to follow his narrative. But the cop has spent enough time with this vet to understand what the guy's trying to say. He's learned to speak the vet's language. The cop knows he can find this guy most mornings sitting in an isolated corner of Starbucks, sifting through the hundreds of magazine photos he has cut and pasted into a collage and laminated. The vet will show his work to anyone he can, even strangers, and the cop has seen the images time after time after time, but he always acts as if he's never seen them before. Why not? It gives the vet joy. Most strangers avoid the vet if they notice him at all. His beard's unkempt, he's lost most of his teeth, and he goes on weird rants. But he notices everything. Which means this vet is a great source of "intel" for the cop, filling him in on all sorts of happenings around town: the guy running one of the popular eateries is using again; the older woman who lives in her car was assaulted and robbed by another homeless man (the vet asks if the cop can check on her). Knowing the vet, taking the time to befriend the vet, makes the cop a better cop.

That's community policing.

The vet also suffers from severe post-traumatic stress, and when his demons become unbearable, it's the cop he turns to. The vet's afraid. He's been thinking of killing himself. It's the cop who calls the VA, then drives the vet to the emergency room, staying there with him until they can find him a bed in the VA hospital a few hours north. Afterward, it's the cop, who on his day off cleans out the vet's efficiency apartment, the cop who finds the rolls of hidden money the vet has hoarded over the years. The cop who deposits that money into the vet's savings account before the landlord hauls his stuff to the dumpster. For months, and then years after the vet is gone, living in a veteran's home in another state, the cop continues to get phone calls about the vet's doctor appointments because the cop is the vet's only emergency contact.

This is not a fiction.

This is community policing.

And there's no graph for this kind of work, no letters of commendation or "points" in the department's system that tracks the officer's productivity. There's no box to check on the quarterly evaluations, nothing that can ever account for the hours and care and concern the cop has given to this vet.

Community policing is also walking through the local library every week, especially during the height of winter or summer, when the weather is extreme. The homeless gather here for the heat or the air conditioning, along with the free Wi-Fi. As long as they're sitting up, they can drop off into sleep, which they often need. For some, this is the only time they feel safe enough to sleep at all. I ask these men and women how they are, and if I don't know them, I introduce myself, not as Sergeant Letonoff but as Vic, the way I'd introduce myself to a friend. I tell them if they need anything to let me know. And they do. They come to me when someone threatens them or when one of them is missing.

That is community policing.

Or this: I'm sent to a routine complaint about a car blocking a driveway. The start of summer, and it has been a slow morning. The home is a three-story beach house that looks to have three driveways, though it's not clear where they start and end. Two cars are parked in front of the house, but I have no clue which one is actually blocking a driveway.

I call up to two young girls on a second-floor balcony and ask if they know which car is the problem. Several adults come out on the balcony and point to the vehicle with a vanity tag.

Man, I think, *I could have made the same mistake.*

Still, the easiest thing to do is to just tow the car and move on. Not my problem, right? Instead, I say to the residents, "This is confusing; I feel sorry for the owner whose car I tow." One of the residents says they aren't going anywhere soon, so if I want to, I can try to locate the car owner before towing. The young girls tell me they saw the people heading to the beach: a mother and father with brown hair and a little boy.

Again, I'm tempted to just tow. But what the hell. I head for the beach, stand at the top of the dune, and survey the crowd. No fucking way, I think. This is impossible — seems like everyone has brown hair and a kid — and on top of that, it's ninety-something degrees, full-on humidity. Sweat rains off of my forehead, and unlike those on the beach wearing bathing suits and shaded by umbrellas, I'm clad in heavy combat boots, dark BDU cargo pants, a fifteen-pound gun belt, and a weighty tactical vest that I wear outside my black T-shirt. I'm drenched with sweat. Again, the little devil in my head whispers, "Man, forget it; just tow the car."

I trudge onto the beach and stop by various groups, asking if any of them own a station wagon with such-and-such vanity tag. I'm not having any luck, but as I go from group to group, people start to comment; they're amazed that I'm taking the time to find the owner rather than just towing the car. They're smiling and thanking me, and yeah, it feels good. After a while, I go to the lifeguard station, borrow their megaphone, and as I walk between the scattered beach parties, I blast through my megaphone, "May I have your attention, please? May I have your attention, please?" I feel like an idiot. "Will the owner of a green station wagon with such-and-such vanity plate, please see me."

After about the fifth announcement, a thirty-something-year-old man with a French accent runs up to me, saying the car is his. I tell the French guy he has to move it, he's blocking a driveway. As we're heading back up the beach, I'm startled when people start to cheer and call, "We back the Blue!"

I did a good thing that day. But I didn't do it for the accolades. I did it because I had the time and I felt bad for the guy.

That is community policing.

It's not a compelling story, it won't make the news, and if not for my recounting it here, no one (except my wife, the French dude, and the people on the beach that day) would ever know it happened. And maybe that gets to the heart of my irritation with your "coffee with a cop" events and "police nights out" where you and the politicians mingle, big smiles pasted on your faces as you hand out coloring books and serve free hot dogs and sodas. Again, it's all fine, but those are one-time deals. Community policing is about hundreds of small, simple acts that, more often than not, are never noticed or acknowledged.

Not by the public.

And certainly not by you.

Because real community policing doesn't equal stats and quotas and pie charts and bar graphs. It's not a photo op or a sound bite.

Community policing is also about the older woman who lived alone on a street that in the offseason was especially quiet, perhaps only one or two houses on the entire road that were lived in. Driving by on patrol, I'd see the flicker of her TV in the front window. She often called the police department late at night, almost always in the dead of winter, the loneliest time in our town. She'd complain that she smelled gas or she'd heard a noise outside. She wasn't the nicest woman — brusque, condescending — she'd make it a point to let us know how successful she'd once been. Whatever her worry was — the gas, the strange noise — we never found anything. After a while, I realized she was lonely, incredibly, crushingly lonely, and craving human interaction.

As my colleagues and I got to know her, we learned she had no family, her meals delivered by a charity. My corporal, Susan, and I started stopping by late at night during the slow winter months, just to check on her. I remember her showing us her scrapbook one night, as she'd been a renowned journalist. Other times we'd just sit with her for fifteen or twenty minutes, watch TV with her, have a cup of tea, let her tell us stories.

That's community policing.

But do you remember what you did when you learned my corporal and I were stopping by this woman's house? You, the same admin that's hosting all those "Coffee with a Cop" events at the library, posing for pictures with the international students?

Yeah, exactly: You sent out a memo telling us to cease these visits to the old lady.

Why?

Well, fuck that. I still stopped by. Just kept it on the down-low. That's community policing too.

As the essayist Leslie Jamison writes in "Layover Story," "This is how we light the stars, again and again: by showing up with our ordinary, difficult bodies, when ordinary, difficult bodies might need us. Which is the point — the again-and-again of it."

That's community policing, the showing up, the again and again of it.

I was watching the door. It was a habit I had and not one I was likely to change. I was a cop. I was aware of these things even when I wasn't wearing a uniform or driving my patrol car. I couldn't turn it off, and I didn't want to.
— *Whiskey & Ribbons*, Leesa Cross-Smith

14

Letter to My Wife About My Cynicism

I know you love me.

I know you admire me.

I know you worry.

And I worry about you: You're the one who, for half the month when I'm on night shift, has to sleep alone in a house that sits on an acre of land with nothing but farms and trailer parks nearby. You're the one tiptoeing around while I try to sleep during the day.

I know your sacrifices.

But I also know I irritate you.

"Stop," you'll say when we're driving around on my day off, running errands. "You're not on duty." I've probably just pointed out the expired license plate tags on the cars we're passing as we head into the grocery. I can't help it. My eyes are trained to see this. Or maybe I've just commented on the lone man sitting in his car near the dumpster at the edge of the parking lot. What's he up to? Or maybe it's after I've pointed out, from a block away, the couple loitering at the entrance of the boutique hotel at the quiet end of town. *Yup, had that pegged*, I might say out loud as we get closer. This couple are definitely junkies: underweight and unkempt with tangled hair and dirty clothes. I see all this in a second, and I know it long before I can articulate it. Even if I say nothing (and I've learned to keep my mouth shut), you can always tell what I'm thinking as I instinctively steer you away from the couple.

You call it "cop eyes."

It's your way of describing this ability to understand, in an instant, a dozen minuscule clues that reveal the "real" story. It's not a good thing in your mind. Cop eyes could just as easily be called cynicism, or distrust, or suspicion.

How many times, getting out of the car as we're headed out for a run on the wooded bike trail just outside of town, will you glare at me when I reach for a jacket to cover your purse, left in plain sight on the passenger seat? You think just because the car is locked, your purse is safe. But sooner or later someone will break out the car window and steal the purse. It happens all the time: purse gone, money and credit cards gone, a broken window.

"I've been an adult a long time," you remind me, "and no one's ever broken into my car."

"You've been lucky," I say.

You call me a cynic.

And maybe I am.

But being a cynic is one of the things that brings me home to you each night. And that's all that matters: Pulling up in our driveway and seeing you at the door, hair in a ponytail, reading glasses perched atop your head, still holding whatever book you were reading, index finger marking the page.

Speaking of books, you were the one who found *A Professor's Street Lessons* for me. It's written by George Kirkham, a criminology professor who was critical of police and became a cop in part to justify that criticism. Here's what he had to say about cop eyes: "As someone who had always regarded policemen as a 'paranoid' lot, I discovered in the daily round of violence which became part of my life (as an officer) that chronic suspiciousness was something a good cop cultivates in the interest of going home to his family each evening."

Something a good cop cultivates.

Going home to his family each evening.

When we go to a call, whether it's a minor traffic accident or a domestic dispute or an argument over a parking space, most of the time we don't have much information. We don't know how the situation came about and we don't know anything about the people involved: their relationship, if they're intoxicated or on drugs, if they're prone to violence, have a criminal history, hate cops. We don't even know their names at first. That's our reality; you know this. Which is why, before the era of body cams, from the very beginning of our training, it was ingrained in us to put our hand on the trunk or rear bumper of any car we'd stopped or had been called on to investigate.

Why?

Simple. Our handprint made us part of that crime scene.

We were there.

No matter what transpires — if we're shot, assaulted, kidnapped, and stuffed into a trunk — our mark stays. If we disappear, left in some never-to-be-found grave, our handprints will leave a ghost clue.

Tangible proof. Irrefutable evidence.

We were there.

I remember the first time I told you this. We'd been married six or seven years and had been together for more than ten. We were in Charleston, sitting in a Starbucks and I was writing this chapter. When I read this part to you, you stopped me, your own hand clamped to my wrist. "Wait, you really do that?"

"Every time I approach a car."

Your face fell. "But that's awful. That you're thinking that way, that . . . They actually teach you this?"

It surprised me that you didn't know. Surprised me that it made you so sad.

Maybe they no longer teach this. Probably not. These days with high resolution digital radios, body cams, and in-car cameras, the need for the handprint is less relevant, but it will forever remain a permanent piece of cop culture. And it will remain a reminder of how much is uncertain in our world, how much we can't know, sometimes until it's too late.

This is why we develop cop eyes.

Every time we walk into a building or approach a car, we're picking up signals that might not only protect us but will maybe help us resolve the situation peaceably for everyone.

A guy surreptitiously jerking up one side of his pants: He might be carrying a gun.

A traffic stop, and I see a woman bend down as I approach: What's she hiding under the seat?

I roll up on a fender bender, and one of the drivers is pacing in the median, head down, clearly angry — not just upset, but angry.

We don't have to act on the signals, but we do have to see them.

Do you remember the day we were walking the bike trail, getting in our ten thousand steps, enjoying being outdoors? It was an unusually warm April afternoon, new blossoms and budding green leaves just arrived, and we were both in a good mood, talking about the usual — our kids, our parents, our lives. And then that middle-aged guy with a backpack rides by on a bike wearing too-large jeans and a flannel shirt. Oh sure, he might have been a college professor, his backpack full of student papers . . . except there's no college nearby. I mumbled "loser" as he passed.

Jesus, you were pissed. "Why do you always make snap judgments like that? Maybe he's just poor. That doesn't make him a loser."

"True," I said. But I knew that most middle-aged guys riding a bike for transportation who aren't wearing Lycra or gym clothes are probably riding the bike because they've lost their license to a DUI. Ninety percent of the time.

After this exchange, we were silent. I felt your anger with me, your dislike, the good mood of the walk suddenly soured. I was horrible, you were thinking, I was judgmental and unfair and this is why people don't like cops. And I was contributing to the stereotype by being a cynical suspicious asshole. I felt bad. Maybe you were right. I was just about to admit that okay, maybe I wasn't being fair, when there he was.

The trail ended near a park and bicycle dude was sitting on top of a wooden picnic table in the shade of a large oak, legs crossed. In an effort to prove that I wasn't a complete jerk, I said to the guy, "Hey, how's it going?"

And sure enough, he takes a long toke off a joint, hoists a beer can into the air, and says, "Just smoking some dope and drinking some beer."

It was all I could do not to burst out laughing.

You were even more furious.

But bottom line? I was right about the guy. Not because I'm a cynical jerk, but because I've got cop eyes, and I've been trained by the job to see what the rest of the world doesn't notice.

Maybe it doesn't want to notice.

I think of how you, a writer who teaches fiction writing, often has students tell you after they've taken a class or two, "You've ruined reading for me! I can't just read for pleasure anymore." They now notice the various writing techniques, see the clunky transitions and clichés. Pure escape into the story is no longer possible.

Having cop eyes is similar. In a way, the pleasure of just walking down a city street on a beautiful day is no longer mine. I'm hyper-vigilant; I can't not be. And sure, this is a burden because a lot of what we're trained to see is ugly. But cop eyes are also a tool. It's like my ballistic vest, my baton, my gun belt. I'd never think of going on duty without these things. And I'd never go on duty without my cop eyes either.

That said, I get that there's no use for cop eyes at home. So, I'm trying to leave them at work. Clearly, I'm not always successful. It's easier said than done. Unlike my vest or gun, my "cop-way" of seeing the world is a part of who I am now.

I think this is why I've fallen in love with gardening. Planning each year what I'll grow in what bed, researching how to grow the best crops. It forces me to notice, pay attention to, study a wholly different aspect of the world.

This year, for the first time, I've planted purple potatoes. I sat at the kitchen counter with you, researching them. We learned that they're called Peruvian potatoes, and that they're twice as healthy as your regular potatoes (which means you won't be raising your eyebrows every time I fry some up with my eggs). Apparently, these potatoes need a lot of nitrogen in the soil and grow best at high altitudes. We live at zero altitude, but I want to try. I love those little suckers. So, I'm curious and excited — which is the second-best thing about gardening (the first is cooking with food I grow on my own land with my own hands).

When I'm gardening, the world gets bigger. I notice things that never registered before: How big zucchini leaves are and how fucking prickly — who knew? How good dirt has lots of worms, melons need sandy soil to keep from rotting, and if my tomatoes get too much water, they'll split. In other words, I'm developing "farmer eyes." It's a counter-measure to the cynicism. When I smell my basil plants before I get close to them, when I notice the first grape-sized watermelon, I feel an energy, a gratification, a joy that the most adrenaline-fueled night of police work can't replicate. In the summer, when you pick me up from night shift — have I told you I love that you drive me in to work on those nights? — and we arrive home, my eyes barely open, my feet dragging, I still take a moment to walk out back to my garden, to check on my plants. "How you guys doing?" I ask them.

I'm hoping that this ability to give my cop eyes a rest not only makes me more well-rounded, but makes me a better man, a better father, a better friend, and mostly, a better husband to you.

Like a lot of attractive women, she regularly drove over the speed limit, secure in the knowledge that every policeman who had ever stopped her for speeding, had given her a warning rather than a summons.
—"Alice, Off the Page," *The New Yorker*, Calvin Trillin

15

Letter to the Young Cop Who Insists Everyone Be Treated the Same Regardless of Circumstances

Imagine a sunny beach day, and you've just pulled over a raven-haired beauty with a sexy Southern drawl. She's in a high-end convertible, and she drives like no one else shares the road with her. Of course, she's speeding. But she bats those big dark eyes at you, then kneels on the front seat — in her very short dress — and reaches into the back to retrieve her purse. She tells you she's not from around here, just visiting.

You remind her that a speed limit means the same thing no matter where she's from.

Or maybe it's not summer. Maybe it's a cool March night, stars luminous in the black sky, people out strolling, taking their time instead of darting madly from their heated cars into their homes. Winter is finally over. A black Mercedes runs a stop sign. The middle-aged driver, with a touch of silver in his hair and a golfer's tan, shakes his head and says in a flirtatious tone, "Damn, you got me." He's already got his license out, and yeah, he's polite and charming, but you can tell the charm has worked before, probably many times.

"Oh, by the way," he tells you, "I went to high school with the chief." He calls him by his first name. "How is he?" he asks. "He treating you right?" Mr. Charm reminds you that he's a local, not just another "touron." He rolls his eyes conspiratorially as he says this, and casually mentions that he owns the largest real estate company in the county.

You remind him that stop signs apply to locals, too.

Look, you're going to come across beautiful, powerful, well-connected people every day, people who already have numerous advantages in life. You don't begrudge them — you've had your share of advantages too. But if you're going to cut some people a break, why not offer it to those who least expect it? Why not give a warning (rather than a citation) to the grumpy old woman with a coffee stain on her T-shirt? Or the nerdy kid who reminds you of the high school misfit that got stuffed into his locker. Who knows? Maybe that misfit was once you. Do you remember how it felt to not fit in no matter how hard you tried? Or give the warning to the anorexic-looking girl with shoe-polish-black hair, nose ring, and black fingernails. Sure, she has a fuck-you-I-don't-give-a-shit attitude, but something in the way she holds herself tells you she's frightened.

Surprise them, Young Cop.

You have a lot of power, and with that power comes responsibility to also have compassion.

These are people you're dealing with; they're not just speeders, tickets, points in some quota that will make the admin happy. Don't forget that. This is a routine traffic citation for you, but for the person getting the ticket, it's not routine at all. It may embarrass or anger them. It might be the proverbial last straw in someone's lousy afternoon. For many, maybe most, it will screw up their day. *I got a fucking ticket*, you can hear whoever it is tell his spouse when he gets home that night. *Why the hell couldn't he have given me a warning? Just once! Christ! This is the last thing I needed today.* You can hear it, can't you? You've maybe said those words yourself, or heard some version of them. I sure have. My wife is a great driver, but her lead foot — I've given up trying to say anything to her. And I don't blame the cops for one minute who don't give her a warning.

But the drivers who make a single mistake, misjudged the light, really didn't notice the speed limit had changed . . . why not?

Yeah, I know. Many people will find fault with you for making any exceptions at all. Maybe you find fault with it yourself. You probably believe if someone runs a stop sign and gets a ticket, everyone who runs a stop sign should get a ticket. No exceptions, no excuses, no breaks. Everyone gets treated equally under the law. I can hear you now, Young Cop, so certain in your conviction, and though I want to admire that conviction, I don't.

You think this will make you a better cop?

It won't.

This isn't to say I don't get where you're coming from. This power of discretion is the area with the greatest potential for discrimination and abuse. Like it or not, we, the police, are the gatekeepers of the criminal justice system, which means that we decide — long before lawyers, judges, or juries — which "criminals" are brought in and which "criminals" are let go. There's little supervision of this, and almost zero oversight. There can't be. Our jobs entail too many unrelated, ill-defined situations.

This is tricky, dangerous, even. I get that too. We all know the problem with making exceptions: There's always the asshole who will use this power to enact his own brand of racism. Black guys who speed get a ticket, while White guys get a warning; Blacks who are disorderly get arrested but Whites are urged to "take the party inside." It happens. It happens more than it should, and it's never okay. But in my experience, what most affects an officer's decision to arrest isn't about race; it's about the attitude of the suspect. (And yeah, this is problematic too: To say that African Americans don't have a lot of reason to feel respectful toward the police is the understatement of the year, and even if it wasn't, no one's legally obliged to show respect.) But cops are human beings too and anyone — Black or White — who is belligerent, rude, aggressive, or argumentative, isn't likely to get a break.

Sorry, but that's not about racism. It's just not.

If I roll up on two scruffy-looking males loitering outside an upscale hotel in the early hours of the morning and I ask, "Hey guys, what's going on here?" and they answer, "Fuck you," I'm going to respond with a hell of a lot more authority and guard than if I ask, "Hey guys, what's going on here?" and the answer is "Nothing much, officer." Neither response is satisfactory and neither answers my question, but as former NYPD police officer Ed Conlon writes in *Blue Blood*, respect is ultimately a matter of safety for a cop. Someone who's resistant and rebellious is a threat, plain and simple, for their "loss of control can escalate into violence."

All we can do is try to be fair, question our motives, be vigilant of our motivations. In doing this, I often err on the side of caution. I think of how, during the last contentious presidential election, I stopped a car for speeding well over the limit. It's bumper was plastered with stickers for the party I did not favor, so I made it a point to issue a warning rather than a citation just to make sure I wasn't being biased.

But again, why make any exceptions at all?

Because in the end, the possibility for benefit in the use of discretion is far greater than the potential for abuse.

Again, it's not just laws we're dealing with.

It's human beings.

Let's say the person who ran that stop sign missed it because she'd just gotten fired from her job; her mind was in a thousand different places, none of them good.

Or his girlfriend just broke up with him. He's reeling. He didn't see it coming any more than he saw that damn stop sign.

Or maybe the guy running that sign was worried about all the ordinary crap we all worry about: his child is struggling in school or business is slow or he's got a new boss who's twenty years his junior without half his experience, and every time he has to ask this child for permission to do something, there's a knife in his gut. Or maybe she didn't sleep well — there's too much to do, not enough hours, and life sometimes feels impossible.

The bottom line is that no one was hurt running this stop sign, no damage was done, and now and then, giving someone a break for no other reason than to make their day a little bit brighter, a little less traumatic, is valid — and valuable. Although the law might say that all people running the stop sign should be treated exactly the same, that it's the same offense every time, I disagree. The person who runs that stop sign because she was texting? She's different. Texting is purposely irresponsible and I'm sorry, but she's getting a ticket. No question.

Here's the thing, Young Cop: Our job would actually be easier if we made our decisions based solely on the law. Why make things complicated? Our job is to enforce the laws, so we enforce them. End of story.

But what if it's not just a traffic violation we're talking about?

How about the most common type of disorderly behavior, public drunkenness? As I've mentioned, I work in a beach resort. People come here to vacation, to have reunions, to get married, and 95 percent of the time alcohol is a key ingredient. On any given weekend when the weather's nice, I encounter wedding parties cavorting on the boardwalk, often with open containers of alcohol, which is against the law. Sometimes the bride is still in her wedding gown and the groomsmen are still in their tuxes, sans bow ties; they're laughing, reliving the day, maybe reminiscing about the things that brought them together. They're boisterous and happy, a little too loud maybe, but no one's complaining. The other pedestrians follow the party with their eyes, smiling, maybe calling out, "Congratulations!" and even applauding as the couple passes. A Saturday night, a three-quarter moon, the slow crashing of the waves in the distance. For the newlyweds, this might be the most important day of their lives.

But they've got open containers, and the law is the law, and they're breaking it.

No excuses, right?

No exceptions.

But I'm not going to issue tickets for those open containers. I'm just not. How would this help my community? How does it protect the citizens? How does it do anything except sour someone's wonderful day? Why not just congratulate the bride and groom and politely ask them to either pour out their alcoholic beverages or take them inside?

That's discretion, Young Cop.

And it's not just your right to use it.

It's your duty.

*He thought being a cop, a great cop, the best cop, meant setting clear, specific,
unbendable rules and regulations for himself and everyone in his life, really
everyone in his city, and never yielding one inch. But that's not how
the world works. Pretending that it does helps no one. And it
makes everyone despise you — the people you're policing,
the actual human beings in your life, the world at large.*
— *Lloyd McNeil's Last Ride*, Will Leitch

16

Letter to the Young Cop Who Still Insists: The Law is the Law, No Exceptions

Let's try this scenario:

A summer afternoon, and I get called to a store that sells kitschy beach stuff: cheap jewelry, T-shirts and sweatshirts with the town's name on them, coffee mugs, and stickers. The owner is holding a fourteen- or fifteen-year-old girl whom she caught stealing a sticker. It's worth maybe ten cents and sells for a buck. But in my state, theft is a Class A misdemeanor regardless of the value of the stolen item: It can be a penny or it can be $1499.99. Any theft, under fifteen hundred dollars, is one step below a felony.

When I arrive at the store that afternoon, the girl is very frightened and very polite, and the best solution, I think, would be for the owner to ban the girl from the store and for me to take her to the station, call her parents and have them pick her up. Punishment enough.

But the store owner wants the girl arrested, and that's the law, cut and dry, black and white. No part of me thinks — for even a second — that the offense should result in this young, foolish girl having a criminal record for the rest of her life, but that's irrelevant.

There's a victim: the store owner; there's a crime: theft; and there's a perpetrator: the girl.

When I send the girl's warrant to the judge, she asks incredulously, "Do you really think it appropriate to saddle this girl with a lifelong criminal record for this?"

"Look, I'm on the same page," I say, "but it doesn't matter what I think. The victim (store owner) wants the girl prosecuted, and that's the victim's right. It's out of my hands."

Luckily the judge says, "Well, it's not out of mine, and I'm not signing the warrant."

I send the girl home with her parents and that's the end of the story. I'm grateful for that judge, and no doubt the girl and her parents were too. Most people (perhaps not the store owner) would agree the judge used proper discretion in choosing not to prosecute, and most people, I would guess, have no problem with the judge's using it. Perhaps because she's a judge.

But unlike most bureaucracies where discretion is greatest among higher-ranking officials, in police work, it's the lowly patrol officer who uses discretion more than anyone else. Why? Because in addition to enforcing the law, we're also responsible for maintaining order, keeping the peace, and preventing crime by keeping an eye out for suspicious activity. And it's with these activities that there's the greatest room — and perhaps the greatest need — to use discretion.

Along with our right to use force, our use of discretion is the most powerful right we have. How we use it can have life-altering consequences.

Let's say I stop a guy whose registration is expired. His car isn't old, but it's not new either. He's wearing jeans and work boots, and his large scarred hands, dirt under the nails, suggest he works in construction or maybe landscaping. It's only mid-morning, but he looks exhausted. He's got a Styrofoam coffee cup in the cup holder. When I run his tag, I discover his license is suspended; he hasn't paid a number of traffic fines. And it's not the first suspension on his record. When I ask him, "Hey, what's the deal with all the suspensions?" his shoulders slump and a flicker of frustration crosses his eyes.

He explains that he got some traffic violations and fell behind on his payments, so his license was suspended. But he needed to drive to get to work or he'd never be able to pay the fines. He got stopped again, and was issued another fine, this time for driving with a suspended license, and now he can't afford to pay that.

And he still has to get to work.

Waves of defeat, helplessness, and anger are rolling off this guy, and I don't blame him. If he can't break this cycle of getting fines and not being able to make the payment on time, he'll be designated a habitual offender and will eventually lose his license for up to five years. This guy can't get out from under; he cannot catch up. So, when I stop him, am I really going to give him yet another ticket for driving with a suspended license? That's the law, after all.

But I have discretion.

And I have a heart.

I'd love to send this guy on his way — his car's insured, he's not a danger to others; he's simply buried in the bureaucracy — only I can't just cut him loose, not in this litigious society. I have to cover my own ass. But I can make his burden less, charge him with "driving with no valid license" instead of "driving while suspended." The former is a twenty-five-dollar fine, not nearly as serious or as costly, and it has none of the repercussions that accompany a "driving with suspended license."

Why wouldn't I give the guy a fighting chance?

Why wouldn't you, Young Cop?

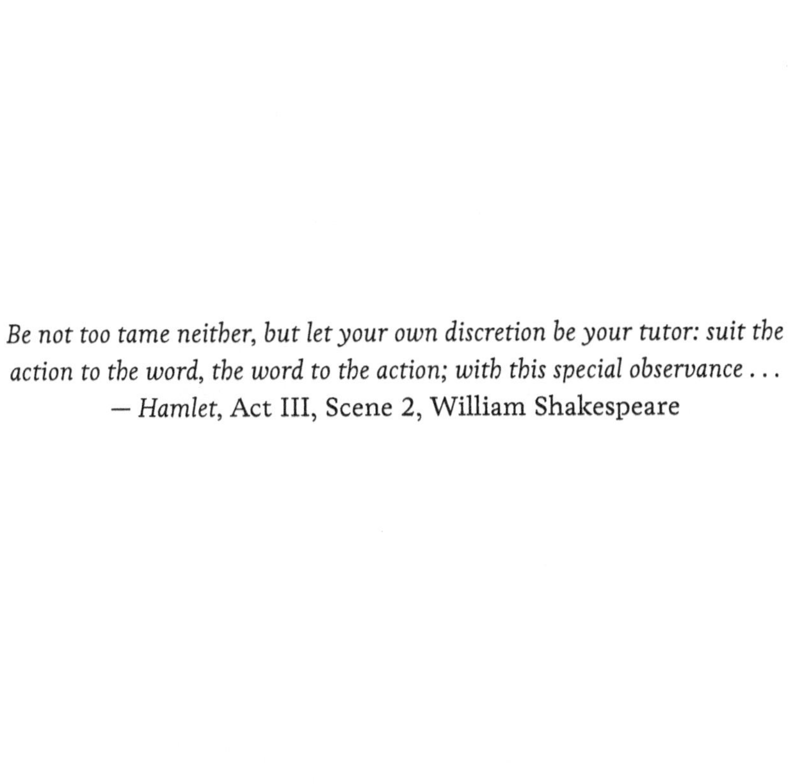

Be not too tame neither, but let your own discretion be your tutor: suit the action to the word, the word to the action; with this special observance . . .
— *Hamlet*, Act III, Scene 2, William Shakespeare

17

Letter to the Single Mom Whose Child I Didn't Take to Child Protection

It would have been much easier, and a lot safer for me, to just go by the law books. But I'm glad I didn't because when I look back on my time as a police officer, this incident with you and your daughter rises up as one where I was at my absolute best.

You were living in an efficiency apartment — it was actually a row of six rooms in a seedy motel on the edge of town. Single-story cinder block, the building's probably been there since the fifties. It's adjacent to a Royal Farms and a laundromat, its parking lot small and cracked, a lone tree growing in the middle of it. The rooms, each with a cheap plastic lawn chair outside the door, are rented by the week or month. You lived here with your ten-year-old daughter who, though functional, was considered by her school to have special needs, requiring a lot of extra help.

I often sat in one of those plastic chairs talking with you; you looked after another of the motel residents, a disabled and reclusive Vietnam vet who suffered extreme PTSD, and I was grateful for your kindness to this man. I'm not sure why your life had gotten so hard — you'd been raised in a middle-class family, you told me, your parents were lawyers, but for whatever reason — whatever mix of circumstance and choice — your life seemed mostly a series of struggles. You looked tired on those days we sat talking, and I knew you worked a number of odd jobs (in a chicken plant, at the Royal Farms) to support your daughter with no help from her father. I'd ask how you were doing, how your daughter was doing, how you were making ends meet. I knew you worked hard, knew you were barely getting by, knew you loved your daughter but sometimes had to leave her by herself at night for a few hours while you worked your shift at the convenience store around the corner.

You were doing your best.

One frigid winter night, I was dispatched to the motel for an intoxicated disorderly female, and when I arrived, I found you standing in the parking lot wearing a fake fur coat, opened in the front, with nothing underneath. You were holding a three-quarters empty bottle of vodka and screaming obscenities. Your daughter, eyes wide with fear, was peering through the partially opened front door of your unit. My heart fell. Your behavior clearly violated the law: disorderly conduct, indecent exposure, and most damning, reckless endangerment, for you were in no condition to care for your daughter.

Maybe the right thing to do would have been to take you into custody and call Child Protection. Simple solution, and who would argue with it? Plus, it was near shift change, and I wasn't in the mood to stay past the twelve hours I'd already worked. But I knew you. I knew you weren't prone to drunkenness. I knew you were a good mother, and I knew something had set you off, no doubt exacerbated by the days upon days of endless worry, mindless repetitive labor, lack of financial and emotional support — and loneliness, unrelenting and overwhelming.

So, I made a judgment call. And yeah, I knew it might come back to bite me, but it was the right thing.

I pulled you into your motel room and had my corporal take your daughter into his car to prevent her from seeing any more of you in this state. The girl was hungry, and so I asked my officer to take her to McDonald's and get her a meal. Meanwhile, I called two women I knew from social services, who found a safe place with a friend of yours where you and your daughter could stay the night until you sobered up and came to your senses.

You and I never spoke of that night, never had a need to. I only know that in the years since you never had a repeat offense.

I'm proud of how I handled that call. I followed my heart, rather than the rules. I can't always do this; I don't always do this. It puts me at risk, a different kind of risk than the danger I might face in breaking up a bar fight, a different kind of risk than what I encounter when, with gun drawn, I approach a vehicle driven by a man with felony warrants. It's not a risk I think the public understands, maybe not a risk you understood either. How could you?

In his wise book, *Letters to a Young Doctor*, the writer and surgeon Richard Selzer writes: "There can never be enough hearts and lungs to teach a doctor his business. Do not rely upon the X-ray machine, the electrocardiograph or the laboratory to tell you what your hands, eyes and ears can find out."

So, it is with police work: There can never be enough hearts to teach a cop his business.

He was not a man who enjoyed confrontation, despite the training,
the badge and what it meant.
— *We Begin at the End*, Chris Whitaker

18

Letter to the Dad Whose Day I Ruined

There are times when no matter how big our hearts, no matter how much we want to help, we can't.

And shouldn't.

That was the case with you.

A busy summer weekend, and you'd come to the beach with your daughter for the day. Driving home, you ran into the back of another car while in traffic. This wasn't a major accident, and you waited calmly for us to arrive. You were Hispanic, a nice man, but you could barely speak English. Your daughter, who was about ten, was fluent in English, and she took control of the situation, acting as your translator. The problem was you had no license, your car wasn't registered to you, and when I asked for the insurance card, your daughter said quietly, "Oh, my mom and dad were short this month, and couldn't pay for insurance."

Fuuuuck, I thought.

Wrong answer.

In the state of Delaware, you must have insurance to drive a vehicle. Had you handed me an expired insurance card or told me you couldn't find it, no problem; I could have completed the accident report and sent you on your way. "Make sure you bring that valid insurance card when you go to court," I might have reminded you.

But now that I knew you didn't have insurance at all? That was a whole different story. I had no choice. I had to impound your car. No way could I let you drive home no matter how much I wanted to give you a break, and I did. You were a nice man, you were there with your kid, and it was hot as hell out. But you lived two hours north, and had you gotten into a serious accident on the way home, I would have been liable for your driving without insurance. And God forbid if you killed someone, robbed a family of their own bread-winner. No insurance, no way to make reparations. Who do you think they'd come after?

Me.

And rightfully so. Because I could have stopped you from driving, and I should have, and I chose not to.

So, I couldn't take that risk — no matter how small it was — not only for myself but for anyone else you could potentially harm.

When I told you I was going to get the car towed and you needed to phone someone to come get you, you began weeping and berating me. "Fuck you! You are bad man! Who are you? Asshole, fuck you!" An endless cycle all the while you were weeping copiously. Your daughter just kept rubbing your back saying, "Poppi, don't worry. It will be okay, Poppi."

You continued sobbing. Although your English was poor, you were fluent in profanity. "You not have a daughter, motherfucker, motherfucker," you shouted at me. Tears streamed down your face.

I felt horrible for you. I do have a daughter. The sergeant I was working with that day has a daughter. And we both wished we could have turned a blind eye and sent you on your way.

You eventually called friends to come get you. In the meantime, it was a scorching day, traffic barely moving, waves of heat rising from the sunbaked asphalt as people headed home, sunburnt and sandy, their cars loaded with boogie boards and beach paraphernalia. You were sitting on your cooler, T-shirt drenched in sweat, sobbing, refusing to allow us to take you to the police station to sit inside while you waited for your ride. Over and over, you just sobbed, "Fuck you, motherfuckers, you got no daughter."

But the sergeant was good. He said, "I do have a daughter, so for your daughter's sake please come back to the station and sit in the air conditioning until your friends come."

Finally, you agreed.

You were still sitting in the silent lobby, closed because of COVID, as I left after my shift. You were subdued by then and thanked me as I was leaving, but driving home I felt awful. I'd basically ruined your weekend, and I felt a little ruined myself.

This is the flip side of discretion — those times we wish we could use it, and we can't.

*He had wanted to keep the death and the killing away from her and
the children, had wanted one place that was normal
and unspoiled.*
— Police Captain Bennie Griessel in *Seven Days*, Deon Meyer

19

Letter to a Young Cop About the In-Between Ordinary

People don't call the police when things are going well. As the writer of one manual about police careers said, "Times of tragedy are sometimes the only occasion people meet an officer."

Times of tragedy — or traffic stops. And no one likes those either. Which means that as many times as we're called heroes, as many times as someone tells me, "Thanks for your service," no one wants to see those flashing lights in their rearview mirror.

They're not too happy to see us at their front door either.

We sign on for this, though. Being disliked, being part of people's tragedies. No wonder, then, at the end of a shift, when it's time to be a father or husband or mother or fiancée, the last thing we want to do is talk about those tragedies. And even if we did, how do we begin to describe the grief and degradation and suffering, especially when it's brought on — as it all too often is — by sheer, unimaginable stupidity? People making ridiculous choices. Choices we can't fathom. Like the man unloading his gun in the backseat of a car, mistakenly discharging it, and not realizing he has killed his girlfriend until she slumps over, the bullet having severed her femoral artery. Or the drunk kid who gets kicked out of a party and decides to drive home at night in a truck without headlights and never expects that he just might get stopped on the forty-mile trip. Seriously? One colossally bad choice and that kid's promising future was derailed. It started with his losing his enlistment in the Marines, followed by more fines and more debt and more problems (losing his license, not finishing high school) from which he couldn't crawl out from under.

I'm not sure why these things are so difficult to talk about, but they are. Maybe it's just the senselessness of it, the over and over and over again of the stupidity, the ruined jobs, ruined relationships, ruined vacations, ruined lives, and for what?

"I don't know what to do with it, I don't know how to explain," I said to my wife just last night. *It wears on your fucking soul* was what I really wanted to say, but what did that even mean? And come on, is my job really that unfathomable that I can't explain it to my wife, who also happens to be my best friend?

And let's be real: The truth is that most of what cops do is pretty ordinary and it's not unpleasant at all. Me? I walk the streets of my town and check the properties, making sure a door hasn't been left ajar or the pipes haven't burst in the winter. I stroll through the library, where the homeless congregate. I know most of them by name and I stop to chat. I have school duty at the elementary school during the drop-off and pickup times, and I cordon off streets for special events or if trees or electrical wires are down. I walk the boardwalk, where in the summer dogs are not allowed, and I politely ask people to abide by that law. Typically, this angers them. (*What are you? A Rent-a-cop?* And *Don't you have better things to do with your time?* And *This is what you do for a living? You should be ashamed of yourself!*)

Needless to say, these are not the people thanking me for my service.

Smoking is not allowed on the boardwalk, and I enforce this as well (luckily, the smokers don't seem to feel the same animosity as the dog owners). Twice a month, I wash and inspect the patrol cars, and on night shift, I drive through town and take note of street lights that need replacing. It's tedious, but it's a safety issue. I run radar, and remove trash cans or large debris that have blown into the road. All of this is just maintenance and it never ends, and every patrol cop deals with it. You'd never know it from the news — or cop shows, where we're either shooting someone or involved in a high speed chase — but more than 80 percent of police activities are noncriminal, and only a measly 2 percent deal with violent crimes. Most of what we do is service related.

We also respond to mundane complaints. These can be anything. You'd be amazed at how many people call 9-1-1 to report barking dogs (and now I'm the one dying to ask the caller, "Don't you have better things to do with your time?"), but I have to respond. I also jump-start vehicles, assist when an elderly person falls in her home. (Don't even ask me about the naked nun in the bathtub). I help people who have locked themselves out of their cars or houses, have lost their keys, lost their wallets, lost their children, lost a parent suffering from Alzheimer's. There's satisfaction in these things, Young Cop. These are the good days.

As the surgeon Richard Selzer tells his interns, "Never disdain the common ordinary ailment in favor of the exotic or rare. To the patients every one of his ailments is unique."

So it is for us.

The small details are important.

I also rescue injured seagulls (yeah, yeah, I know), shoot rabid animals, have even cordoned off the beach when a seal washed ashore (to protect the seal from all the people wanting to pet it). These are the stories people love to hear about at parties or when having dinner with friends — all this weird shit no one ever thinks about when they think about what cops do.

We also rouse drunks who have fallen asleep in public, sometimes taking them home if they're local; ditto for the homeless, which involves finding a place for them to stay. We respond to medical calls, everything from heat exhaustion to overdoses to heart attacks. I wish the latter wasn't routine, but for cops, it is.

And then there's the stuff that's not routine, the stuff you do see in Hollywood's version of what cops do: the rapes and arson, the dead bodies, the call about a child who's not breathing (and was already dead when I arrived on the scene). People ask about these things because news of tragedy travels quickly. Still, it's all pretty factual. Who, what, when, where. Clearly defined beginnings, middles, and ends. We begin at point A and go to point B. There's a story. There's a reason. Sometimes there's an answer, even if it's not one we want to know.

It's the in-between experiences that get to me — and will probably get to you too, Young Cop. That dad whose car I had to impound because he didn't have insurance. Jesus, I would have loved to have cut the guy a break. Instead, I ruined his day. And that ruined mine. Or the family who arrived one Friday night to start their week-long vacation. They'd splurged and rented on Craigslist the perfect beach cottage a block from the ocean. They had photos of it and instructions as to where to find the keys. Their car was packed with towels and beach toys, the kids already wearing their swimsuits. But they'd been swindled. The address of the beach cottage didn't exist, and now they had no money, no place to stay. They were devastated and when they came to the cops for help — there wasn't one thing we could do.

Or what about the summer night you're called to the family-owned amusement park for an assault? The place is loud and chaotic — people screaming on the pirate ship ride, bells and buzzers going off at the arcade, the ocean booming in the background, parents photographing kids on the carousel. In the midst of this, a middle-aged couple butts in front of a family standing patiently in line for tickets. The father tells the couple, "Hey, the lines starts back there," and without warning, the woman shouts "Fuck you!" and calls him the N-word, then punches him in the face.

You interview witnesses, review surveillance footage, and when you identify the woman, you spend hours running her name through databases, searching license photographs until you find a picture that matches the surveillance footage. You confirm it's her, get a warrant, but it's served by the guy on the next shift, and you're never called to testify, never hear another word about it. Which means, chances are the whole thing got dropped. It's not unusual. There's no story here, no closure, and in the end, all your work can't undo the damage that woman caused.

Another couple comes to the beach to celebrate their anniversary. They've been married thirty, forty, maybe fifty years. She has the beginnings of dementia. As they're strolling through a brick-paved alley lined with quaint shops and eateries, he has a ruptured aneurysm. After the ambulance takes him away, after the crowd that gathered disperses, after you rinse the man's blood from your hands and uniform — you were first on the scene, even before the medics — you are left with this confused, terrified woman whose husband has just been taken. She can't drive, and he's been flown to a hospital hours away.

You'll spend the afternoon trying to track down a relative who can help her. But there's no one. It's dark by the time you drive to the State Police headquarters an hour away, where someone from Victim Services will meet you to drive her another hour to the hospital where her husband may be dying. That's the real drama: spending hours of your life with this woman in the worst moments of hers. There's no villain, no crime, no justice to be served. There's no training for this, no Hollywood happy ending, no ending at all. But you can't even process this because already the next call is coming in — a domestic dispute or a heart attack or maybe just another damn dog is barking and the neighbors are irritated again, and now you've got to deal with that.

Still, no matter how futile those experiences seem, no matter that you'll never know what happens to that old woman and her husband — you hope to God he's okay, but you can't even call the hospital to find out because of health privacy laws — at least you know that you were the one who figured out how to help that woman when no one else was there. There's a sense of accomplishment in this, a sense of pride in this ability to take whatever's thrown at you and find the fix. That woman might never know your name, just as the family who was swindled won't, just as the guy you brought back from an OD won't, just as the woman whose boyfriend rapes and beats her won't, just as most of the people you help won't. But your life will have intersected with theirs in the moments when no one else was there. This is no small thing.

Hold onto this, Young Cop, even on those afternoons when you save someone from an overdose only to hear that the same person had overdosed the day, the week, before. Hold onto it when the guy you just arrested for driving under the influence of narcotics shows up at your house to drop off his son who, as it happens, is friends with your son. At dinner that night, his kid won't look you in the eye.

There are thousands of these small, awful, ordinary moments, and they accumulate, lodge inside us, emotional bullets that leave scars. I think of the winter night when the medics were trying to get a man dying of bone cancer into the ambulance, and he was sobbing, begging us to stop his pain. It was my last call of the shift. I left to go on a second date with the woman who would become my wife. I didn't say anything about the experience, not because I couldn't, but because I didn't want the tragedy of that man's pain and the ugliness of his illness and my own sorrow to seep into the rest of my life.

These are the kinds of things I wish your parents, your spouse, the public could understand. They have no idea what we do; they have no idea how much we do. It's not the robberies or the criminals that take their toll. It's the daily, ordinary despair we are called upon to witness, and that, by the nature of wearing the badge, we say we are willing to witness. The stuff no one else wants to see.

Jesus. Do these people have any idea what they're saying when they're yelling about defunding the police? Do they have any clue what will be lost?

What we would learn that night, and in the years to come, is that you get thrown into a situation without understanding all the pieces — like entering a movie already in progress — and all you can rely on is your gut instinct, experience, and if you're lucky, the officers around you. And only after it was over could you piece together what had happened and why.
— *Anything You Say Can and Will Be Used Against You,*
Laurie Lynn Drummond

20

Letter to Those in a Cop's Life Who Wonder What Changed in Their Cop

Most folks don't see a lot of graphic trauma during their life. The exceptions are combat soldiers, emergency room people, medics — and cops. Think about rubbernecking. People don't actually want to see whatever it is, but they do sort of, you know? Morbid curiosity. Cops, on the other hand, have to see it. That's the job, really. Seeing, dealing with, what nobody else wants to deal with.

So, somewhere near the beginning of our careers there's going to be an event — something awful, something unimaginably ugly — that flips the switch in our psyche, allowing us, afterward, to be the "Cool Hand Luke" of crisis. The event may not be the first or second or third fucked-up thing a new cop deals with — I went through a few things before my switch was thrown — but somewhere in the beginning of our careers, an event stands out and becomes the defining moment. It happens to us all.

The Before.

And the After.

I'm writing to you because if it hasn't yet happened to the cop you love, it will, and you need to understand it. Or maybe it's already happened and you see that he or she has changed: There's a quietness in him or you'll hear her sigh, brace her shoulders as if getting ready . . .

For what??

I think back to a conversation I had with my friend, Jason, who started out as a rookie cop in Kentucky.

"Probably my second day on the job as state trooper," he tells me. "I was working in a very rural area. Rolling hills with narrow little roads winding around lush fields and dense forests, horses in pastures, goats and cattle, and dilapidated single-wides with years of accumulated junk decorating weed-filled yards. My thought when I got assigned to rural Kentucky was *what can possibly happen here?* Let me tell you, every fucking thing happens there, with the poverty, the dope and the violence, it's all there in spades, man.

"Like I said it's my second day, and I'm with my FTO [field training officer], a seasoned trooper with a lot of years under his belt. We're dispatched to a residence; an elderly lady reported she'd hit a deer. We pull into her driveway where her car is parked. And draped across the hood is the deceased body of a human, not a deer — a human. Its head is through the windshield; it's her neighbor. The poor bastard decided to get his mail at the wrong time and got clipped by Miss Daisy. Remember, it's rural Kentucky with windy roads, blind corners, and no shoulders.

"I was twenty-four years old, my second day on the job, I'm dumbfounded; actually, I'm in shock. What was really astounding to me was the old lady could not process that she'd just whacked her neighbor. In her mind, she had struck a deer, and there was no way to convince her otherwise.

"I couldn't believe what I was witnessing. I just stood there watching my FTO. He was as calm as a warm June day, not the least bit fazed. Matter of factly, he took her statement, all the while 'Yes, Ma'am'-ing her, jotting down notes, and giving her the occasional 'uhm-um' and 'I understand.' After he finished up, I was still numb. I said to him, 'Holy shit, man. How were you able to remain so calm and collected? How can you do that?'

"He paused, gave me a closer look, then said, 'Give yourself some time; you'll understand.' "

Jason and I are both old cops now, and we do understand, but I'm not sure our parents, our spouses, our friends ever did, and I wish we could have explained what had happened to us, in us. Bear with me; I'm going to try.

My second year as a cop, I had my event. Even now, more than two decades later, I can hear the gunshot in the predawn darkness, see the body on a small jet of sand near a soon-to-be-busy highway.

"New guy?" the old cop says to me. "Run down and see if he's dead."

Mid-autumn, comfortable but not sticky. The wind is still. The water doesn't move.

I stand next to the body of a once-young man, his hand holding a high-powered rifle.

"Yeah," I tell the old cop. "He's dead."

Sadness befalls me.

The quiet unsettles me.

But it wasn't his death, or the brutality of the scene, that changed me. It was the open twelve-pack of cheap beer near his body and the footprints visible in the sand from his pacing. Two of the beer cans were empty and another, partially full, stood on top of the cardboard case. What haunted me was knowing that in the last moments of his life he paced; he cannonballed two beers, gulped from a third, then made up his mind. It was the thought of those lonely, horrifying minutes that made me, on that day, want to be the kind of cop that can witness this level of sadness, carry it, and keep doing whatever needs to be done.

Every cop will eventually have that moment or that detail that they can't shake. It haunts them. It changes the way they see the world.

A neighbor, a bright Kentucky morning.

A half-drunk can of beer.

A switch gets thrown and can never be thrown back. There's a recalibration inside, an acceptance of what happens every single day, somewhere, whether most people know it or not. We do. We know ordinary human beings will face unspeakable horrors. It's not about right or wrong or judgment or blame. We can't stop or fix or change the awful thing — it has usually happened by the time we arrive. Our job is to absorb the unimaginable so that the world can slowly begin spinning back to a place that makes sense again.

They talk about the call of duty, but what is it that makes the call of duty so pressing?
— Wind, Sand and Stars, *Antoine de Saint-Exupéry*

21

Letter to My Father About Duty

It's been over a year since you left us, Pops, though I'm glad you did, because I know you were suffering, and it was hard, those last years, watching you fade. Every day you seemed to become more translucent. People would ask, "how's your dad?" and I'd say, "he's hanging in there," but you were more ghost than anything else.

Unless I brought a military guy by to visit.

If I did that, your eyes, dulled by sickness and age, would immediately spark with attention. It happened the last time with Robbie — do you remember? One of my son's high school buddies. Robbie is a Marine recon special operator, and as you and he exchanged stories of training and military operations, I imagined I saw a white flame shimmer behind your pupils. That was maybe a year before you died. By then, you mostly slept or stared out the large glass panes beside your bed and watched the squirrels. I used to study your gaunt face, your frail skeleton, and I'd wonder what you were remembering.

I've been thinking about you a lot, and about your father, my grandfather, who flew a French Nieuport biplane for the Russian army in the First World War when he was still in his teens. His brother, also a pilot, was killed in that war. Later, after the war morphed for the Russians into the Bolshevik revolution, and your father's mother and sister were murdered by the Bolsheviks, your father fled to Constantinople (now Istanbul), where he joined the French Foreign Legion. Eventually, he found his way to America, enrolled in the University of Pennsylvania, and became a pathologist. He wasn't yet thirty.

And then I think again about you. I can't not these days. It's August, the birthday we always celebrated together (because they're just two days apart) fast approaching. You would have been ninety this year.

In your mid-twenties, you became an Army ranger, setting the stage for your tour in Vietnam. As a new captain, not yet combat-tested, you were sent into a raging battle to take control of an armor company that had lost both its commander and second in command. You were dropped off by helicopter down the road from the conflict. Night, surrounded by jungle, walking alone. You were inexperienced and scared to death, you told me. But you rose to the occasion, rallied your troops, and were subsequently awarded the Silver Star for Valor. Fuck, Dad, how did you do it? And I can't help but wonder: Could I have been that kind of leader, could I have been that brave?

And in the next breath, I'm thinking of those seventeen-year-old kids storming the beach on D-Day. Seventeen years old and charging into machine gun fire. Jesus! But they did it because they believed it was their duty and because they believed in duty itself, the concept of duty. And because they would face disgrace at home if they didn't fulfill that duty.

It worries me, Pops. Sometimes, I fear the concept of duty has become old-fashioned. I mean, could D-Day have happened in the kind of world we live in now? A world filled with safe spaces and trigger warnings? When did we become so fragile? When did we lose our sense of duty? Duty, from the late fourteenth century, *duete*, meaning "the force of that which is morally right." How does one learn this? *The force of that which is morally right.*

How did you?

I suspect you'd tell me that it has to do with decisions, with being capable of making difficult decisions. It has to do with independence, and with having a strong sense of self. I guess I worry that in the world we inhabit today, where too often a sense of self is dependent on others — how many friends on Facebook, how many likes or dislikes, how many social media followers — it's getting harder for young people to acquire this sense of self.

You would have called it a sense of duty.

Like most young men when the time comes to leave home, I left thinking I didn't need the "old-fashioned" values of my parents, the gifts of character passed down from each generation. How was it then that a sense of duty and honor overtook my youthful flightiness and folly? Why now, as a cop, do I run toward those things — choose to run toward those things — that everyone else is running from? Why do I crawl wearily from bed, exhausted after only four hours of sleep following a grueling sixteen-hour shift, and return to duty once again? Why do I feel this overpowering sense of service? And how can I pass it on not only to my kids, but to the young cops I now train?

Dad, it was your example of what it is to be honorable and duty bound, to have a character with a compass that is true and unwavering that guides me. And so all I can do, all any cop can do, is set similar examples. To show up not only when we have to, but when showing up is the right thing, the necessary thing to do.

Yesterday, along the highway in the late afternoon with the August sun beating down, I saw the glare of red and blue lights from a police cruiser in the distance and figured it was a fender bender, maybe just a speeding ticket. But no, it was a cop on his knees changing a tire for what looked like a group of college kids. I was proud of him, Pops. I think you would have been too.

He had it: that sense of duty.

It has become appallingly obvious that our technology has exceeded our humanity.
— Albert Einstein

22

Letter to a Young Cop About Technology

The world my father and grandfather knew was so different from the world in which I became a cop, and how vastly different that world is from the one in which you have become a cop. Just think of all the technological advances in our field (I like saying *our* field to you, Young Cop). We now use lasers to measure a vehicle's speed, wear body cams that record what really happened, have endless and massive intelligence data at our fingertips, and can instantly know the criminal history of anyone we encounter. Our crime reports are fed into programs that predict future crime probabilities: where and when the next drug deal will go down or the probable location of the next purse snatching. The point is that our technological resources are awesome, almost unfathomable.

But no matter how much our lives have been altered in amazing ways due to the wild and miraculous innovations in technology, the ability to think quickly, make rapid-fire decisions, and communicate face to face remain your greatest assets.

In other words, technology has nothing to do with what will make you a good cop.

Technology has nothing to do with duty. Yeah, I'm back to that: *the force of that which is morally right.*

I know, I know, this seems counterintuitive. We live in a world, and you came of age in this world, where the prevailing attitude is that technology equals progress. And believe me, I like a lot of this progress. Every time I use Google Maps to help me navigate a new city, I honestly can't fathom how the hell I ever got around without it.

Still.

To even suggest — and okay, I am — that new technologies are not better than the previous ways is to be old-fashioned, behind the times, backward, a dinosaur, which is how I often feel. But reviews of technology and policing mostly conclude that technology has not significantly improved our performance.

If anything, technology — specifically, the telephone, the two-way radio, and the car — has done a lot of damage to our profession.

Try to imagine the time before any of those things were invented.

"When I first became a policeman," said Superintendent W.J. McKelvey at the third annual National Association of Chiefs of Police in 1896, "nobody dreamed of telephones and patrol wagons then . . . an officer was forced to lug his tipsy prisoner on a wheelbarrow for miles sometimes to the station."

I'm hard-pressed, as you probably are, to see an upside to this. And yet having a car, for all the good it did, forever changed how cops engaged with the public. Before cars, cops were an integral part of the community. And because we were alone, we had to know how to talk to people. If a cop encountered an unruly suspect, there wasn't any backup, no way to even call for backup, so he sure as hell better have learned to talk to that "suspect" as just a regular guy. And because this was his "beat," because he'd been out walking the streets day after day — instead of just showing up when there was a problem — he probably knew the guy. The cop would use this guy's name, speaking to him not as an authority, but as just another dude. "Hey, Joe, what's up?" he might ask. "What's going on?" He'd smile; he knew Joe, knew where Joe lived, knew what kind of trouble Joe could cause.

He knew how to talk to Joe.

Yeah, this might sound old-fashioned — and okay, it is old-fashioned — but it works, and if it ain't broke, don't fix it.

Something similar happened to me not that long ago. St. Patrick's Day weekend, the weather was nice, and after a year of lockdown due to COVID, the bars were finally open, packed with people drinking way too much. We got a call from one of the bars that a huge, ex–pro football player was looking to fight. *Here we go*, I thought. *Fuck!* But the officer I was working with knew the guy, had played Pop Warner football with him when they were kids. "I've got this," he told me. And he did.

Young Cop, we've discussed this: You're not going to spend most of your time on patrol chasing criminals. You're just not. Dispatch data, taken over the course of a year, from the Wilmington, Delaware, PD revealed that officers spent only 50 percent of their shift enforcing the law. Fifty percent. That's it. The rest of their time they dealt with order maintenance and public assistance (jumping cars, giving directions), traffic control, and medical calls. And most arrests weren't made for violent or property crimes but for smaller "crimes of disorder," basically public annoyances: drunks who can't find their way home, fender benders, noise complaints. I not only have twelve-hour shifts where there's not a single arrest, I have twelve-hour shifts where there's not a single call for anything — not even a complaint about a barking dog!

So, I walk the streets, chat with store owners, run by the Starbucks to check on my Vietnam vet. In my small town, I know who has chronic illnesses or Alzheimer's, who has kids with disabilities, who the drunks are. I even know who's likely to make a noise complaint or call the chief when a construction worker begins work before eight a.m. And because I know these people, I know how to handle them without force.

Treating people as people and not as problems to be solved is one of the most important things you can do. Even with strangers. You can change a person's day because of some small act of assistance, and this, in turn, might change that person's life. Helping an old woman unlock her car on a scorching summer morning after she left her keys inside rather than just handing her the number to a locksmith, finding shelter for a homeless man on one of those January nights filled with sleet and wind, driving a tourist around the packed streets of your small resort town when he can't recall where he parked. Technology can't do any of this, Young Cop. Sure, it can help locate the shelter, perhaps the lost car, but it can't replace the sense of duty that will drive you to act even when you don't have to.

Duty: *the force of that which is morally right.*

Technology can't replace kindness.

We were prepared for encounters with strangers in ways that the digital age would buffer a lot us from later.
— Recollections of My Nonexistence, Rebecca Solnit

23

Letter to a Young Cop About Communication

You know what else technology can't replace, Young Cop?

Good communication skills.

The ability to connect with people is what makes one cop extraordinary and another just a guy in a uniform.

Don't be a guy in a uniform.

When my wife and I first started dating, she lifted my gun belt to hand it to me as I was getting ready to head out. We'd only gone on a few dates, and I had stopped by for a quick cup of coffee before starting my night shift. "You've got to be kidding me," she said, as she listed to one side, trying to heft my belt to her shoulder. "No wonder you have hip problems." She set it back on the table. "I can't believe you run in that! How could you possibly catch anyone?"

Fifteen years later, I'll still overhear her telling people that story: how astounded she was the first time she lifted my belt.

Yeah, our gun belts are heavy. They weigh between fifteen and twenty pounds, and hold the tools of our trade. My belt is a thick leather strap, and attached to it is a large handgun in a holster with a twelve-round magazine inserted into the handle, plus one round in the "pipe," making it thirteen rounds. I wear a Taser, pepper spray, two more magazines of ammunition, two sets of handcuffs, a digital radio, a case containing rubber gloves and a universal tourniquet. That's a lot of stuff. The tool that's most important, though, the tool that weighs nothing, yet carries the most weight, is the tool of talk.

It should be a cop's most valuable asset.

It is mine.

And this isn't just some politically correct, let's-make-the-public-feel-good crap. Our ability to talk to a variety of people in a variety of situations is crucial for our safety. Way more important than our guns or our vests.

Last night our town was off the rails with drunks and noise and adolescents and chaos. A young biker I'd seen before was in town. I'd noticed him because I love motorcycles, I've built them, and have been riding since I was twelve. In a lot of ways, this guy was a biker cliché: long hair, tattoos, no helmet, bad-boy attitude. He reminded me of myself at that age — reckless, invincible, eager for whatever comes. Women in their twenties, wearing cowboy boots with their miniskirts and halter tops, flocked to this guy.

As I pulled up to an intersection, he came flying around the corner, with one woman riding behind him with her legs wrapped around his waist and another woman sitting in his lap, facing him, with her legs also wrapped around his waist. It was a sight to behold, and if I were thirty years younger, I would have loved to have been that guy.

But I'm not.

I'm a cop.

Immediately, I put on my lights. He was already pulling over. We had made eye contact as he rounded the corner. I just shook my head at him and he nodded. He knew. The women jumped off, scampering away. Our young James Dean sauntered toward me, grinning in a "yeah, yeah, my bad" kind of way.

"Really, man?" I said. "I get it. You're having a good time, impressing the women and all that, but here's the problem. If someone fell off and got injured, that's not just a traffic violation; that's reckless endangerment, dude."

His face went pale. "I never thought of that," he said. "Honestly, I was just in the moment."

I could have been a hard-ass. I could have ticketed him for reckless endangerment, ruined his "being in the moment" moment, but why? I could tell he wasn't going to do this again, in part because the last thing he wanted to do was hurt one of those women. In the end, I got what I wanted. I didn't have to crush his dream or embarrass him to do it.

Remember, Young Cop, our goal is to get the suspect to do what we want, and persuasion is always the best method. Sure, force is an option, but it damn well better be the last option.

I know you know this.

You don't want to use force either. None of us do.

So, we need to talk to people. Just talk.

Take, for example, a DUI arrest. There's no wiggle room, no discretion: You drive drunk, you get arrested. End of story. Too many lives have been shattered because of drunk drivers. This means that by the time I ask, "Do you know what the legal limit is to drive?" (and most drinkers know it's 0.08 BAC), the repercussions of the arrest have already been set in motion: loss of license, no way to get to work, maybe the loss of a job. There's the embarrassment and the cost of the arrest. And if it's the third DUI, it's a felony. Most felons will lose their professional licenses: doctor, pharmacist, lawyer. In other words, there's a lot at stake with these arrests, and drunks can be volatile, especially if they start thinking about the potential consequences of the DUI. A smart cop knows this, and knows that the more the drunk focuses on what's happening, the more difficult and dangerous he can become.

Hey, man, you'll get through this, I often tell them. *Even grandmothers get DUIs.* Or *Just cooperate with me, and we'll get you home as soon as possible.*

These things are true. There's no reason to use deception.

What kind of work do you do? I might ask in an effort to get them talking about something, anything, else. I ask if they have kids or are married, where they're from, if they grew up around here. Depending on what they say, I'll ask other things, try to keep them talking, try to keep the conversation going.

Again, I don't say anything that's not true, but I'm trying to deflect their attention away from the severity of the arrest. My mission? To get the job done with as little drama as possible. It's that simple. And this isn't just about saying the right words, but how you deliver those words, how you look at the person, your tone, your attitude, your empathy. Even with something like drunk driving, which causes so much sorrow and grief, in that moment when you've taking the drunk into custody, you need to remember that he's is in a bad place. Lecturing, talking down, using sarcasm — how is that going to help? And again, this isn't touchy-feely, bleeding heart shit, Young Cop. We have a job to do, so why not get it done in the most humane way possible?

In the same vein, I always keep a pack of cigarettes with me. I don't smoke, and I wish no one did, but many of the people I arrest do. And if they're familiar with the system, they know what's in store for them. There's no smoking in jail. The fact that I have a cigarette when they start jonesing changes their attitude, calms their nerves. My job gets easier, and their anxieties are tamed. Again, it's a simple matter of my recognizing that I'm dealing with a human being, not just a drunk, a domestic abuser, a thief, a junkie.

And empathy goes both ways. I'm more than a cop. I too want to be recognized as a human being.

Why is that so difficult?

I think one of the biggest political failures, and the biggest social failures,
over the past few years has been the failure of empathy; not being
able to look at the other person down the street.
— "Talk of the Nation," NPR, June 26, 2012, Colum McCann

24

One More Letter to the Young Cop About Communication (It's That Important!)

For the most part, Delaware's a rural state. Except in the north, the roads are two-lane county roads, and it's not uncommon to be stuck behind enormous combines or trucks transporting live chickens to the processing plants. These areas are mostly conservative, and the majority of the residents don't think twice when encountering armed citizens, which isn't unusual because Delaware is an open carry state, meaning civilians may carry firearms as long as they're not concealed.

However, along Delaware's Atlantic Coast, the industry is tourism, with visitors from New York, New Jersey, and the Washington, DC, area flocking to our beaches. For them, seeing ordinary citizens strolling the streets carrying guns causes alarm and fear.

One July weekend a young couple who were practiced Second Amendment advocates — they knew all the legalities and rights afforded them in the state — decided to provoke a police response by strolling the beach with pistols dangling from their bathing suit clad hips. And of course, a police response was quickly generated. Anxious calls came pouring into our 911 center about dangerous-looking armed subjects on the beach. *Here we go,* I thought. Someone has to make a constitutional rights stand on my watch.

Sure enough, I found the couple walking the beach, zigzagging through the crowded groups of sunbathers, families, teenagers playing paddleball in the surf. I felt everyone watching me, waiting to see what I'd do, maybe feeling relief (it's one of the few times people might have been glad to see me). I was aware of this, but here's the thing: The couple wasn't doing anything illegal.

Aside from being openly armed, the couple had a hard look. Both had long unkempt hair and their torsos and arms were covered with black ink tattoos. The man was lean and muscular and the woman was thin and sinewy. They were primed for me, ready to strike with legalese and attitudes.

"How you all doing today?" I said. I was smiling. It never hurts to start this way. I understand why police officers don't smile — they feel a stern demeanor helps establish their authority, but the uniform already does that. And smiling often disarms whoever you're talking to.

"It sure is hot out here in this uniform," I said. "Unfortunately, I don't have the option to wear my swim trunks." I smiled again. "I guess you know why I'm here."

"We know our rights," the woman said. "And you can't ask us shit, Mr. Policeman."

She was right; I couldn't even ask for an ID because again, they weren't doing anything wrong.

"Hey, I got you, man," I said. (I call everyone "man," even my wife.) "You're absolutely within your rights. In fact, I'm on the same page when it comes to the right to bear arms. But look around you. The majority of these people are from areas where guns are more regulated; I'd bet most of these folks have never touched a gun, so the only thing you're doing is scaring the shit out of them. The worst part is that it's a summer weekend, the beach is packed, and I've got only one other certified officer working with me today. So, if you guys continue to march up and down this beach with your pistols exposed, the 911 center will be bombarded with calls. And since I have to respond to every one of those complaints, this means I'll be doing nothing all day but coming up here. I won't be answering other calls that may be priority. So, as thoroughly as I respect your right to bear arms, you guys are going to wear me out." Truth is, I was already worn out. Drenched in sweat, thirsty, exhausted.

I'm sure it never occurred to them — the logistical problems their stand was creating for my small, overburdened police department. And how the hell could they understand unless I explained where I was coming from?

All I know is their demeanor completely changed. They dropped their guard. I could see they felt badly for me. Suddenly, I was not *the* man, but just a man, trying to do his job.

"How about we put our pistols in our car and make this stand on another day?" the guy said.

Everything we do, Young Cop — from asking someone to walk on the sidewalk instead of the middle of the street or dealing with fights over parking spaces or fender benders, or a young James Dean showing off on his motorcycle, or a school teacher getting a DUI — everything starts with a human being having a problem or causing a problem.

Our job is to solve that problem.

And the better we can communicate that this is our goal, that this is our only goal, the more likely we'll be able to do just that.

I remember how when I first married Matt, I was wary of even telling people he was a cop — all of the stupid assumptions they would make about him.
— We Are Not Like Them, Christine Pride and Jo Piazza

25

Letter to My Wife About Why People Don't Want Cops Around

Today, I was reading Rosa Brooks' memoir, *Tangled Up in Blue*, about becoming a cop. Early in the book, describing a discussion about an orientation meeting, she spoke of the "genial," welcoming officer and then followed the description with, "this guy was much too nice to be a cop."

I put the book down. *Too nice to be a cop?* What does that even mean? I know it was just a throwaway line, and maybe she meant it to be funny, but I was struck again by how pervasive — and accepted — it is to stereotype cops. The suggestion is that, at the most basic level, we aren't even decent human beings.

Here's another quote about a cop, this time from the novel *The Damage* by Caitlin Wahrer:

"There was something about him that made it easy to forget he had children of his own. Grown children, grandchildren, judging by the pictures in his hallway. It wasn't his personality that made her forget — it was his profession. There was something about him being a detective that made her forget he existed outside of that."

Again, two sentences, and it's just fiction, made up, not even real life, but it stopped me. I handed the book to you.

Is this really how people feel?

And okay, I get that most people don't actually know a cop, and if they've interacted with one, it probably wasn't a positive event. Probably, it was a traffic stop — speeding, running a red light, illegal passing, using the cell phone — it can be any of a thousand things, but the story is the same: The person's been busted for doing something she shouldn't have been, and even if she's like you and was just pulled over for doing 70 mph in a 35 mph zone, even if she knows she's wrong, even if the cop is polite and explains why he has to give her the ticket, she's not happy. And more than that because there's something a little traumatic about getting pulled over, the flashing lights coming up behind you, the other drivers rubbernecking. There's shame there, maybe fear: the heart racing, adrenaline dumping.

No one wants to get stopped by a cop.

No one. Not even you.

And on top of that, the stop isn't a single event. There are repercussions: Maybe the person is now late for whatever she was racing to get to. The insurance premiums are going to increase, she might get points on her license, and let's not forget the hefty fine. In short, that person's day is, if not ruined, certainly soured, and all that negativity? Bingo! It gets associated with the cop.

Without him, the day would have gone along just fine.

You know all this, of course, but you love me, you see the guy beneath the uniform, and so no matter how many times I've tried to explain it to you — cops are in the business of saying no and who the hell likes to be told no — you still couldn't fathom how much people don't want to be in the company of the police.

That all changed — do you remember? — the night you and your friend Ginny came into town for a drink while I was on duty. It was winter, and the town was empty, the party season over. The crowds of visitors were long gone with only a few cars parked here and there along the main avenue of the town. The holiday lights had been taken down and most businesses were closed. The distant boom of the ocean was the only sound.

You and Ginny were at the Purple Parrot, a popular bar that from time to time in the midst of the chaotic summer season needed my professional assistance. You wanted me to come in and say hi, but I told you no. "Bars don't want cops inside unless they call for them. Trust me on this."

"But there's no one else there," you insisted.

"Doesn't matter," I said.

Still, against my better judgment I went in to say hello, and true, no one else was in the bar. But within moments the bartender came over and said, "if you're taking someone out of here, take them out, then please leave!"

You and Ginny were clearly startled and I could tell you felt embarrassed for me. You were also angry. "Seriously?" you asked the bartender, your eyes hard, but I just shook my head, apologized to the guy, and left. I was angry at myself. I know better. A cop in a bar, unless he's there to break up a fight or haul out a nasty drunk, is bad for business, and God knows, these bars are desperate for business in the offseason. All it takes is one potential customer to look in the window while I'm there chatting with my wife, and he decides to move on. I've cost the bartender a sale, not to mention a tip. And even if the bartender had called for my help, the only reason would have been because there was trouble.

No one calls us when things are going well.

It's that simple.

Why then am I still surprised when I read those lines in a novel: *Too nice to be a cop?*

Why does it still sting?

*For you yourselves are fully aware that the day of the Lord will come
like a thief in the night.*
— 1 Thessalonians 5:2

26

Letter to a Young Cop About Being the Opposite of a Hero

And then there is this — the flip side of the good we do, the flip side of everything I've said about kindness and having good people skills. Sometimes doing our duty isn't kind or caring or empathetic at all, and we've got to live with that too.

Sure, we do some great things. We're the ones who do CPR on the heart attack victim and help the scared dementia sufferer find his way home.

But we're also "a thief in the night." We show up to take someone's father, son, daughter, mother, husband, or wife away. And yeah, we're doing that because they fucked up and there's consequences — there has to be — but to the family we're just some assholes in uniform stealing their person. We come and crush their world. Remember that, Young Cop. It's also part of the job.

Picture one of those mornings: a mid-Atlantic late winter, cold but not freezing. It feels damp but it's not wet, maybe because the sky has that color like an off-white dull blanket that rounds the edges of everything. An older model dark-colored Chrysler rumbles by as you sit in your parked patrol vehicle. The Chrysler's muffler doesn't sound so good and the driver just gave you "the LOOK." The look is hard to describe but most cops recognize it. It screams, "Something ain't right here."

So, you follow the Chrysler. It takes a route that doesn't make sense: pulling into the bank parking lot only to drive out its exit, then going a long circuitous way to get to Main Street when a simple left turn would have done the trick.

You stop the car because you notice the registration is expired. The car is driven by a thirty-something man with his young son on board. More problems pop up: The child isn't buckled in, and he's standing in the front seat next to his dad. You see the kid watching through the rear window as you approach the car.

The problems compound: The driver doesn't have insurance, the car isn't registered, and it hasn't been inspected in over a year. His license has been revoked, and he has warrants out for his arrest.

This guy isn't going to be taken into custody without a struggle, you can tell — his eyes are darting looking for an escape, he's sweating though it's cold, his lips are tightened, and his muscles tense. You call for back up, and when officers arrive what do they see?

You're struggling on the ground, one cuff on the guy and you're trying to get the other on. Both of you are out of breath and tired.

What else is going on?

The child is watching this unfold from the car. He's crying, snot and tears running down his face. He's confused and terrified. Why are these assholes in uniforms hurting his dad, his hero?

Young Cop, how do you fix that?

You can't.

*The season chiefly for breaking into houses is during winter,
and long nights.*
— "Street Robberies Considered," 1728, Daniel Defoe

27

Letter to a Young Cop About the Weather

This morning, it's taking longer for the daylight to make its appearance. By the time I start my shift the sky is smoky and overcast with a hard wind blowing off the ocean, causing bushes and treetops to sway and jiggle. Blossom petals litter the damp roadways. Fat raindrops fall steadily with the cadence of a slow military march. Although it's well into spring, the temperature is only in the forties, so with the wet and the cold, working in short sleeves isn't comfortable. It's impossible to shake the chill. Not a day for a walk.

Weather.

And yeah, I know, you're probably thinking: *Wait a minute. Weather? That's what we're going to talk about? Seriously?*

How the hell did we get from discussing something like duty, which is at the core of what it means to be a cop, to . . . well, weather?

Geez, can we get any further from the big issues, the important issues? Duty, morality, courage — hell, we haven't even broached the subject of racism . . . and we're going to talk weather? Give me a fucking break. Have any of us ever watched a TV cop drama where the biggest threat wasn't a serial rapist or a murderer or a mob boss . . . but the weather? Talk about a yawn-fest. Or what about reading a police procedural (think of our fictional Jesse Stone, or John Sandford's *Prey* series): Was weather ever the threat terrifying the small town?

No.

Because no one would bother to read that book.

What about the police academy? Did we ever discuss weather?

Doubtful.

Weather is mundane. Weather is boring. It's what people talk about when they have nothing else to say.

But, Young Cop, weather's always been a major factor in the events of man, and it will always be a major factor in your job, and it is absolutely connected to duty and courage and morality and even yes, racism.

Think about it:

In 1588, the Spanish Armada was the strongest naval presence in the world. Spain ruled the sea, was poised to defeat another great seafaring empire: England.

Except . . . You guessed it: weather. Hurricane-force winds off the coast of England basically destroyed the Spanish Armada.

The shape of the world, altered by wind.

Or consider our own history. The American Revolutionary Army was definitely the underdog army, a ragtag bunch of volunteers without uniforms, some without weapons, going up against the Brits, a well-equipped fighting force. General Washington and his men were facing sure defeat at the Battle of Long Island, when on August 22, 1776, a thick fog rolled in and allowed the Americans to slip away under its cover. Yup. Weather. Without it, would the colonial forces have been around to fight another day?

These examples are just two of many. Entire books have been written on this subject alone: history and weather.

Think of D-Day.

Think of 9/11.

No way can you can think weather isn't important. Like I said, it's going to play a major role in your duties.

Hurricanes, tornadoes, floods, blizzards, earthquakes, droughts, landslides, even a heat wave or a strong wind, a dark rainy day

— these things change our lives in small ways yes, but in big ways, too. Take an ordinary snow storm — not a blizzard; just a few inches of a wintry mix, enough to close schools and businesses for the day, enough to make driving treacherous. Suddenly, people who need medical care can't get to it, they panic, and call you; ongoing domestic problems escalate into violence; or a person with dementia wanders out into the snow, and it's a whole different ballgame than if there wasn't snow. Easier to slip and fall, easier to get confused, easier to not be seen. And what if the power goes out? Now people have no heat, no electricity. More panic. And sure, these are basic problems, but they're still problems, and the more severe the weather events, the bigger the problems are. And not just for those you serve, Young Cop, but for you too. You can't get to your mom in her nursing home and she's out of milk or toilet paper or whatever, and now she's calling in a panic too. But you're on duty, and duty requires you to show up for the civilians you serve. They come first, even when it means leaving your husband or wife or children at home, your aging mom.

Duty, Young Cop. I told you we'd come back to that.

Before the fires obliterating large areas of California, one of the worst natural disasters in our century was Hurricane Katrina in 2005. New Orleans was without power, 80 percent of it was flooded (as were most of the police vehicles), and the police radio system was completely shut down. There was no way for officers to communicate with each other, no way to know what to do. They had zero training for this. Zero preparation. Keep in mind that more than nine hundred officers lost their homes — more than 80 percent of the force. Officers from the Third and Seventh Districts had to be rescued; Fifth District officers had to walk out in chest high water; and throughout the city, many officers were stranded on rooftops.

Despite these losses — not to mention the destruction of their homes, the fear and suffering of their family members — these officers showed up for duty. Later, these first responders would be more susceptible to post-traumatic stress syndrome, and numerous officers would become ill from wading through toxic waters during the rescue operation. One officer died from an infection acquired during this event, and two officers committed suicide. Even when it was all over, when the city was struggling to rebuild, officers had to keep showing up. They might not have had a home anymore, and many of their families had been evacuated, but there they were.

And yet . . .

And yet . . .

Although more than thirteen hundred officers showed up for duty, living in their cruisers for days, rescuing hundreds of people, the media focus in the aftermath of Katrina was on the 228 officers who went AWOL. Go ahead and Google "Hurricane Katrina and police officers" and 90 percent of the stories are about either those 228 cops who didn't show up or about the isolated and, yes, egregious cases of police misconduct during the worst of the looting. It infuriates me. Where is the focus on the thirteen hundred who sacrificed their health and the well-being of their families for the sake of their city?

But isn't this often how it goes?

The bad cops are the ones you hear about.

Of course, Hurricane Katrina was the weather exception, but no matter where you work, weather will be an issue. It brings out the best of people, but the worst too. The poorest people in New Orleans, the ones who needed the most help, were the last to get it. This infuriates me too. We all know the story, how class and race were a big part of what went wrong. Oh, these things had been there all along — this wasn't new to the poor and the Blacks who'd been dealing with it for decades — but it suddenly got really clear to everyone else. And the cops had to deal with that too, and it was one more thing they hadn't talked about in the academy any more than they'd talked about the weather.

Chances are you'll get no training in weather-related events, Young Cop. Even in the aftermath of Katrina, 86 percent of New Orleans officers received no emergency response training and 91 percent claimed they'd received no emergency equipment. It's mind boggling: These guys work in a city surrounded by water but had no training — none — in water rescue. The department didn't even have life jackets.

But why am I surprised? I spent twenty-one years working in a beach town, the Atlantic Ocean a half mile from the station. In the nearly two decades I worked there, my department has never trained in water rescue.

We had no equipment either.

None.

And sure, extremely violent storms are rare, but so are "active shooter" events. Why do we train for them and not for weather-related emergencies? I think, too, of Hurricane Sandy (2012) which devastated beach towns only twenty miles north of where I work, and so I know that one day it will happen: My town will be the epicenter of a major storm, and my fellow officers will have to deal with a catastrophe for which they aren't trained.

It's easy to say that major storms like Katrina and Sandy are beyond the scope of small departments. That's what FEMA's for, right? That's what the National Guard's for! But when the disaster comes down, the local cop will always be first on the scene. That's you, Young Cop, and you'll have to do the best you can, doing what you've never before done.

Weather.

I sit here at the end of another shift, one of so many. Today, the smokiness of the sky has changed to a flat matte gray with paler gray clouds airbrushed across its expanse. The rain has stopped, and at the edge of the sky the sun is present but just can't quite break through. The puddles have vanished and the wind has slowed enough so that the trees only sway but no longer jiggle.

On my honor, I will never betray my integrity, my character or the public trust. I will treat all individuals with dignity and respect and ensure that my actions are dedicated to ensuring the safety of my community and the preservation of human life. I will always have the courage to hold myself and others accountable for our actions. I will always maintain the highest ethical standards and uphold the values of my community and the agency I serve.
— Law Enforcement Oath of Honor, International Association of Chiefs of Police

28

To the Officer Who Didn't Show Up for Work

In August 2011, we had Hurricane Irene, and a just year later, "Super Storm" Sandy, and both events involved police-enforced mandatory evacuations. What a mess. I'm sure you remember because as it turned out, the Irene evacuation wasn't needed. The storm missed our town almost completely. So, of course, when we tried to evacuate people a year later during Sandy, they flat-out refused. And not just refused. People were pissed off. Contemptuous. Thought us fools and clowns. We'd made them evacuate for Irene and what a colossal wasted effort that turned out to be. And now, for the second time in just over a year, here we were telling them, once again, they had to leave their homes? No way. Privately, we agreed: If we'd been in their shoes, we wouldn't have evacuated either.

Still, it was our job not only to enforce the evacuation, but to block entry to the town, except for essential personnel. I was positioned at the drawbridge at the entrance to the main thoroughfare into the city, waiting for Sandy to hit, listening to constant updates over the radio. The wind was gusting and right above me were electrical wires, dancing in the wind like jump ropes in an elementary school yard. Jesus. One of the transformers started sparking and flames appeared, but I couldn't come up with a remedy to reduce my exposure if a wire came down. On top of that, I was parked at the edge of a canal (hence the drawbridge) that was fast reaching its capacity. I knew that if we got a big surge off the ocean, the only place I'd end up would be in the drink. Not a good proposition. I started making a plan, looking for contingencies.

The sky was ferocious, painted with low, thick, black and silver clouds, the winds pummeling my police car, my only shelter. The sideways rain was like a thousand pinpricks against my face each time I was forced to leave the car to confront another "Curious George," who, ignoring all the obvious signs that no entry was allowed, wanted to "check out the waves." I'd tell him, "NO," probably saying it several times in several different ways. Back in my car, I was cold, soaking wet, and yes, angry.

As if this weren't enough, tornadoes were spiraling up the beach and the town's warning sirens were wailing. A fellow officer from the town two miles south radioed that a tornado had just passed him and was heading my way. He warned me to take cover, and my skin started to crawl because there was no cover.

I remember watching the sky change from dark gray to green-black, my car rattling in increasing intensity as the wind gusts grew. If the storm hit at or just south of the town, as predictions warned, all hell would break loose. Hurricanes always spin counterclockwise in the Northern Hemisphere, so when one makes landfall in the mid-Atlantic, anywhere north of the eye will get the storm surge. All of us on the shift knew this. The knowledge sparked from us like static electricity, every one of us rolling the "what-ifs" through our minds as we carried out our duties, as we all worked with a little bit of a faraway gaze.

We were all apprehensive. The wind was blowing so hard and the surf violent, and I had to turn my radio way up to hear the dispatched calls. I couldn't remember a time when the sky seemed so ominous and frightening to behold. In the midst of this, you phoned and said you couldn't get to work — some shingles had blown off the roof of your house and you needed to stay home.

"Really?" I said. "Are you going up on the roof in the storm to fix it?"

"No," you said. "But I don't want to leave my fiancée alone."

My stomach knotted. We all had wives, kids, and significant others. I thought of my own fear as I left for work that day, leaving my then girlfriend (now my wife) at home alone. Our house is surrounded by tall pines already bending and creaking in the wind, and thoughts drifted to the possibility of one of them snapping and crashing down on the house. Before I left for work, I took out the propane stove and heater and filled the tub with water so she could cook, stay warm, and flush the toilet if the power went out. It terrified me to leave her, but this is what we do, and you — a veteran cop, a guy I would have trusted with my life — you knew this.

I expect, and the public has the right to expect, that when the time arises when it really matters, a cop stands tall and does his duty, does what's expected, does what he has been trained to do. We all have those times. They don't happen often, but when they do, that's what all the training was for. Maybe it's an active shooter: You don't get to stand outside, behind cover, waiting for additional officers to arrive as children and teachers are being shot. You just don't. Jesus. Each gunshot is a life being extinguished. Or maybe it's the hurricane. Sure, it might turn out to be nothing, but it might not, and you can't take that chance. You think those thirteen hundred New Orleans cops who stood their ground and gave their all during Katrina had any respect for the two-hundred–plus cops that fled their posts? Fuck no.

I lost a lot of respect for you that day and I never got it back. There are times that a cop has to show up, times when no matter what else is going on, he can't call out sick.

No exceptions.

There are no second chances.

The stress of dealing with people during heightened states of emotion could be withering for even the most experienced cops. It could be fatal to a rookie's career. Jesse had seen it in L.A., rookies melting down under the pressure of the moment. Some losing their cool, blowing up at citizens. Others reduced to tears. While others just walked away. Takes a special kind of person to be a cop. It's not about the gun and the badge.
— *Robert B. Parker's Debt to Pay: A Jesse Stone Novel,*
Reed Farrel Coleman

29

Letter to Those Who Believe Social Workers Can Replace Cops

More and more, cops are being called upon to handle issues better dealt with by social workers. We're the ones handling addiction and homelessness; we're the ones dealing with the mentally ill and those who can't afford medical care. This is part of what's gone so terribly wrong with policing, you argue. Social workers are trained to deal with those who have been caught in this net of hopelessness. Cops, on the other hand, too often resort to force, which is not the answer. We need more social workers; we need more people who will show empathy and kindness. Your assumption, again, is that force is our go-to.

But sometimes, it has to be.

Take the clearly intoxicated driver who refuses to get out of the car.

Or the guy involved in a domestic dispute who won't leave the premises, continuing to lunge at his girlfriend, shouting obscenities.

Or the young couple who has been assaulted in a bar, the woman with neck injuries, and her boyfriend keeps interfering with the police and medics, threatening them, trying to grab her, potentially causing more harm. No matter how many times the medics and cops explain to him that they're trying to help her, he won't let up. He's aggressive and out of control.

There comes a point when the time for talking is over.

Some kind of force is needed.

This is never where we want a situation to go.

From day one in our training this was emphasized: The goal is always to talk, persuade, cajole, order, command — whatever it takes — to convince the person we're dealing with to do what we need her to do, without force.

When I was training at the academy and we were learning how to transition from "verbal judo" to the initiation of force, we developed code phrases that indicated enough is enough; the talking's over. A common phase we'd ask a suspect was, "Is there anything I can say or do that will get you to cooperate with me?" If we said this, and the suspect still refused to comply, we would immediately use force.

No, this didn't mean we'd start beating the suspect or spraying him with pepper spray. Typically, officers would grab the uncooperative person, take him to the ground, apply handcuffs and make the arrest. We practiced this so we could do it as quickly, efficiently, and safely as possible. And we didn't always take the suspects to the ground. Sometimes we'd lean him over the hood of his car; sometimes two officers applying pressure to the arms was enough to get the handcuffs on. There was also an element of surprise; it was designed this way to avoid escalated resistance and lessen the chance of injury to everyone.

Normally, this works well.

But there's only so much we can practice. The reaction of the person on whom we're applying force ultimately dictates how much and what kind of force is used. And yeah, just writing that, I already know it's going to piss people off. Sounds like I'm blaming the suspect for whatever force is used.

I guess I am.

Don't resist and there is no force. Period.

The criteria for officers in choosing to use force has always been based on what is reasonable in that specific time and place.

Is it reasonable to demand that a drunk driver relinquish control of his vehicle?

Yes.

Is it reasonable that those involved in a potentially violent domestic situation be separated? (Isn't this better than being arrested?)

Again, yes.

And is it reasonable that a man, though he has the right to be angry and upset, not interfere with the treatment of another victim, even if she is his girlfriend?

Yes.

The problem is that "reasonable" is subjective. And in the wake of too many instances of unreasonable use-of-force incidents, those of you demanding more social workers and fewer cops are also demanding clear-cut rules about what constitutes reasonable. You want to insist, for instance, that it's not reasonable for officers to use force unless the suspect initiates the force.

Sounds good on paper.

Sounds reasonable.

But let's take our drunk who won't get out of the car. He's not initiating force. So, how long is it reasonable for the officer to stand outside the guy's window, ordering him to take his hands off the wheel and get out?

Ten minutes?

Half an hour?

Three hours?

It's not as if we can just walk away. And what if other calls come in? A heart attack, robbery, drug overdose, even a fender bender. Do we not respond to those calls because we're waiting patiently for the drunk to what? Sober up? Come to his senses? Be reasonable?

Can the social worker really handle this more efficiently? Sure, the guy needs addiction counseling, maybe detox, maybe a lot of things including empathy, but empathy ain't going to get him off the road, where he's a danger to himself and others.

Handcuffs will, though.

And what about the domestic dispute? These are among the most common calls police officers handle, which means most cops have a ton of experience, and so they know — it's basic common sense — that if the couple can be separated and given time to cool down, chances are the whole thing will blow over. No one needs to be arrested; the situation will resolve itself. Isn't this the best possible outcome? Keep in mind, we're not talking about domestic violence, but a dispute, an argument that's gotten loud enough that someone called the police. If, in their anger (and drunkenness, which fuels a lot of these calls) the couple can't be reasoned with, and they continue verbally abusing each other, inflaming the conflict, is it reasonable for the officers to let the problem escalate simply because no one has initiated force? Wouldn't removing one of the parties be the more reasonable option, even if this involves putting one of them in cuffs?

And when a woman is seriously hurt and wants medical help but is so intoxicated that she's kicking the medics and screaming obscenities, and her boyfriend, who is equally intoxicated, is trying to push his way into the ambulance, isn't it the most reasonable thing to subdue him, albeit forcibly, and remove him from the already chaotic scene?

This assumption that social workers are better equipped to handle such calls? It makes me ache. It's so misguided, it's so ignorant of how complicated people and their problems are. Remember what the road to hell was paved with?

She wondered which cases would continue to haunt her, years from now.
She considered telling Hendricks not to kick himself, that every
cop inevitably makes a wrong call.
— *The Wife, Alafair Burke*

30

Letter to My Sister-in-Law About Our Mistakes

"It's disgusting," you commented to me a few summers ago after numerous Atlanta police officers had called out sick in the aftermath of a police officer being charged with the murder of a Black man who'd stolen his Taser and tried to shoot him with it. "Good God, it was just a Taser. It's not like it was going to kill the cop."

"Yeah, but if it incapacitated the officer, what was to stop the guy from stealing his gun next?" I asked.

You rolled your eyes. "All I know is that it's a good thing doctors and nurses aren't like that. Can you imagine if they got tired of treating COVID patients and just didn't show up?"

You're a nurse yourself, and I know I've told you before how many times nurses have helped me out — saved me! — when I had to bring a drunk to the ER for a blood draw. I admire their calm and cool. I always felt like we were a team. But you aren't the first to make this comparison between cops and doctors, cops and nurses.

I didn't say anything that day sitting in your kitchen, though I wanted to remind you that although doctors and nurses, especially during COVID, were choosing daily to put their lives on the line, unlike cops, they weren't being shot, weren't having their cars burned, weren't having rocks thrown at them or their families threatened simply for wearing a white coat.

So, it wasn't the first time — and it certainly won't be the last — that I'd heard this comparison between doctors and cops. It makes sense. We really do have a ton in common, starting with the fact that when people come to us for help, it's usually because they have no choice. They're in trouble or pain and they're scared and vulnerable and we're it: the last resort.

Doctors and cops are also first responders, trained to deal with emergencies, and we're on call at odd hours.

We both swear oaths of service, doctors to do no harm, police officers to defend and protect the constitution and "ensure that our actions are dedicated to ensuring the safety of our community and the preservation of human life."

In both of our professions, it's difficult to become certified and equally difficult to lose that certification. And then there's the Good Samaritan law. It applies to everyone, but it's crucial for doctors, nurses, and cops. The law offers protection to those who give assistance during an emergency — the doctor or nurse who stops at the scene of a traffic accident to provide life-saving care or the off-duty cop who witnesses a crime and intervenes. Our skills and training make us uniquely qualified to help in these cases, and I don't have to tell you, we want to help, but we've also got to be protected. We're putting ourselves at risk physically and financially. The assumption behind the law is that whatever happens, even if it goes wrong, our motives were good.

And so it is in our day-to-day jobs. It saddens me that I have to say this to you, but I do: Our motives are good.

We all — cops, doctors, nurses — do our best and it's not easy and we're not perfect, but let me say it again. Our. Motives. Are. Good. I don't know what else I can say.

Maybe because people see it so often on TV shows, maybe because people have been in an ER at least once in their life, they know that an ER doctor, in a single shift, might be dealing with everything from broken bones and asthma attacks to sports injuries and fatalities; from car accidents, to gunshot wounds and rapes. And even without having ever been in an ER, almost everyone has an experience where a doctor has saved either their own life or that of someone they love. We take it for granted that doctors are smart, maybe even brilliant. Their knowledge is vast, their training extensive — the science alone that they have to master is daunting, not to mention the incredible hours they put in, the sleep deprivation, all they give up to become a doctor.

But so it is for a cop. We're wearing a dozen different coats and performing a dozen different roles with a dozen different rules — all within a single shift. And I love this about our job, all the more so because 95 percent of the time we pull it off.

Think about it: Because we have to prosecute minor cases in the lower courts, we have to know courtroom procedures, how to introduce evidence, and argue a case. We're also medics, often first on the scene of an accident or an assault; we're the ones stopping the bleeding, doing CPR, using the AED, clearing the airway of someone who's choking. We act as marriage counselors in domestic abuse cases, as social workers when dealing with kids or the homeless or the mentally ill — and we deal with them constantly. We're bereavement counselors, often the first person family members interact with in the aftermath of a death. We're scientists, analyzing crime scenes, collecting and securing evidence. And our written reports? It's not just paperwork. Every report is a legal document, and the care we take with it can profoundly affect another person's life. Whether a drunk driver with repeat offenses stays on the road or whether a rapist walks free may rest on our ability to clearly articulate the facts. It's daunting. And that's only some of the roles. We're mechanics, helping people get into or start their cars. We're addiction counselors dealing with the drunks or using Narcan to save the life of a heroin abuser two, even three, times in the same week. Sometimes I feel like a damn travel agent, calling the cheap motels outside of town, trying to find places for the intoxicated or abused or homeless to stay.

Why then, given all this, are police officers not held in the same high regard as doctors? We both have the ability to save

— literally save — another human being's life. It's the most amazing and humbling feeling to know that a life would be gone, snuffed out of the world, if not for our intervention. I've done it seven times that I can put my finger on. Saved three people who were not breathing with CPR, brought three people back from drug overdoses by administering Narcan, stopped one young man from committing suicide.

I'm proud of this. God, I'm proud.

But the flip side of this incredible opportunity to help another human being at the level of life and death is that when we err, and we do, it can be catastrophic. How can you, a nurse, someone who understands this as well as anyone, be so judgmental?

All I know is that doctors are forgiven by the general public; cops increasingly are not. This despite the fact that many studies, including one from the National Academy of Medicine, report that each year around 700,000 people in the United States are adversely affected by medical mistakes, and between 44,000 and 98,000 people die from these mistakes. Jesus. Take the lower of these numbers — *forty-four fucking thousand!* — and this still puts medical error as the eighth-leading cause of death, more than breast cancer, AIDs, and traffic accidents. In contrast, American police killed, in one year (2015) 1,146 people. And granted, that's too high — but compared with forty-four thousand? And do we really want to know how many of that number are Black deaths? Do we want to go there? To the fact that Black women are three to four times more likely to die in childbirth — childbirth, for crying out loud! — in this country than White women? That Black patients are 22 percent less likely than White patients to receive pain medication when they need it? And yet you feel contempt for my profession? And people like the activist and writer Rosa Brooks say that the "level of violent death is so high, policing can reasonably be compared to war"? It's absurd. That's like calling the accidental deaths from medical mistakes systemic genocide.

Come on.

I'm not trying to slam doctors here. I'm just baffled: Why are cops under much greater scrutiny and judgment for far, far, fewer mistakes?

Why, when the doctor makes the mistake, do you give that doctor the benefit of the doubt? Even if it was a mistake due to negligence, even if it was a bad decision or poor judgment or inattention or whatever it was, people — you — assume the mistake wasn't intentional, wasn't driven by malice or racism or a lack of care. You assume and accept that doctors are human, that the health sciences aren't exact, that nothing is perfect.

Policing's no different. We make bad decisions, we miss important clues, we misread situations. Not because we're racist assholes, but because we are flawed human beings. And because we are dealing with equally flawed human beings.

Is it that our mistakes are so often performed in the public eye, whereas the mistakes a doctor makes typically happen in a closed environment where she is surrounded by other professionals who understand the nuances of what is happening and why? Is it because there are no cell phone videos in the ER that within hours transform to YouTube clips that go viral?

All I know is that there is out-of-proportion intolerance, rage, and contempt for cops who make mistakes. And it's wrong. No one hates a bad cop more than a good cop, but it's not mistakes that make you a bad cop, it's malice.

There's a big difference between the two.

The police department had been vilified, and she along with it. She'd been spat on, figuratively and literally, by the people she thought she stood for and protected. It was a hard lesson, and a sense of futility had set upon her and was deep in the marrow now.
— *The Dark Hours*, Michael Connelly

31

Second Thank-You Letter to My Seasonal Officers

I keep coming back to the conversation where my friends asked me why I was still doing this job. The answer I gave at the time was, "it's what I know." But in the months of writing these letters, I realized it's a lot more than that.

I just spent the day instructing a new batch of seasonal officers in the use of handcuffs, baton, and pepper spray. I was amazed by the enthusiasm of these young people. In a time when I'm thinking no one in their right mind would consider a career in policing, here they are.

At the start of training, I introduced myself, my experience, my credentials, and my expectations. Then, I went around the room and had each cadet stand and tell me about themselves. Six are women, one is Black, two are Hispanic, one is transgendered. I asked where they were from, their education, and how they see their future. Most are studying criminal justice, but they come to this little Delaware town from a variety of backgrounds: One is an equestrian athlete from Wisconsin. Two of the women are in the military, one getting ready to deploy overseas at summer's end. There's a former high school wrestling champ and a kid who, like me, has juvenile diabetes.

There are only thirteen of them, when typically there would be at least thirty. But thirteen of them were standing before me, faces bright, excited dispositions, waiting in earnest to learn what I had to teach.

Their exuberance is infectious, reminding me of the joy and excitement I once felt for this job, the sense of purpose, the importance of what I did.

And I realize it's still there. I haven't lost it.

They — you, Young Cop — keep me going.

He came to understand that there is always more to tragedies than is narrated, that the narration is never neutral.
— *Tremor*, Teju Cole

32

Letter to the Public About a Cop's Use of Force

In the last few years, there's been a ton of scrutiny — and rightfully so — of use-of-force choices by police officers. Sadly — and oh, so typically — police administrations have responded as they all too often do, by creating a lot of cover-their-ass bureaucracy around a situation that has nothing to do with bureaucracy. I'm sorry, but more paperwork and more forms to fill out and all those graphics and flow charts and new levels of force and new categories of force and new standards of force and definitions of force — it's exhausting, and it's not the answer. It's a pretend answer, a feel-good answer, a look-at-how-much-we're-doing, come-pat-us-on-the-back answer.

And you, the general public, you're buying it without understanding the situation. No big deal, you think, to have all these new policies if it makes our communities safer.

It doesn't.

When I started as a cop, physically taking a suspect down and cuffing him when he wouldn't comply with a verbal command was not considered using force as long as the suspect wasn't injured. This was just a necessary part of the job, and we trained so that we could do this safely and efficiently. No one got hurt. But in the last few years, my department began to consider as force almost anything beyond light conversation between an officer and a suspect. Suddenly there were not only more "levels" of force, but numerous instances of force that had to be documented.

Level One Force (which didn't exist as a category of force twenty years ago) now includes using strong language, giving loud orders, placing a drunk's hands behind his back to cuff him, or displaying one's pepper spray. Not using pepper spray, mind you, just pulling it out.

Level Two Force is force with injury, and it involves actually using pepper spray or a Taser. If a suspect strikes an officer and the officer strikes back, this is Level Two Force; if the suspect falls when running from the police and scrapes his knee, this is also considered Level Two Force.

Jesus.

Level Three is deadly force, and doesn't necessarily involve a gun, but any object an officer uses to strike a suspect.

For example, it could be a car. Any force that can result in death, even if it doesn't, is Level Three Force. If you shoot someone but don't kill him, it's still a Level Three.

Here's the problem with these additional categories of force and with calling something force that really isn't, like yelling at a drunk or pulling his arms behind his back or taking out one's pepper spray (but not using it): Most officers have to do this shit regularly during the normal course of duty. Only now, we have to document this "force," and it becomes a part of our permanent record.

So what? you might think. If everything the cops are doing is above board, what's the problem? And if documenting all force, however minor or however tedious it might be, makes officers more aware of how and when they use force, all the better. If it keeps one more Black kid from being shot by an overzealous cop, well, that extra paperwork's a small price to pay, isn't it?

No argument.

Except, once again, it's not that simple.

In all my years working as a cop, I had very few use-of-force reports. Maybe a dozen total. Think about that: a dozen use-of-force reports in two decades. About one every two years. These incidents included drawing my gun but not firing it, using pepper spray, and defending myself physically when a suspect was swinging, kicking, or trying to bite me during an arrest. With each of these instances, there was a review of my response — as there should have been. To use force is a serious action and I had to be held accountable, and I was, and I never had a problem with this. I understand the need for police departments to be more transparent. I want this. I applaud this. It's good for everyone.

But under the new guidelines, I probably had a dozen uses-of-force in just one year, and I'm sorry, but calling something "force" that clearly isn't (issuing a command in a loud voice) and then obsessively documenting that instance of force, has not made me a better officer and it certainly hasn't made my town a better place to spend time.

It's actually done the opposite.

It's made my job more dangerous, unnecessarily so, and this, in turn, makes the community less safe.

Because if an officer, a good officer, should find himself in the nightmare situation where he does have to use actual deadly force, and if the incident makes it to the media, all you, the public, will hear is that Officer Smith or Jones or whoever he is — had numerous, numerous! — prior use-of-force incidents. And what you'll think — and I don't blame you — is not that Officer Smith had to raise his voice on X occasions or show, but not use, his pepper spray X times. Instead, what you'll think is that this cop had a problem; this cop had a pattern of excessive force.

I can hear it now. *Officer Smith had twenty-four use-of-force reports in just eighteen months! Twenty-four! Why the hell was he still on the streets? He should have been fired after the fourth or fifth use of force. But twenty-four?* There will be talk of police officers covering for their own. *Those cops! They're all the same. Power hungry!*

Because when the story is reported, no one is going to differentiate between the levels of force. No one is going to realize that Office Smith's twenty-four uses of force either involved handcuffing drunks or yelling at people to slow down or step back or raise their arms.

Yelling.

Who's going to take the time to tell that story? No one. Why? Because yelling at someone and slapping handcuffs on drunks is not a story. Twenty-four uses of force, though? That sounds bad, doesn't it? That's a story. And so, the narrative of the overly aggressive power-hungry cop (in dire need of anger management) will get a little louder and a little stronger, and the complicated truth will get buried a little deeper.

If we make force about everything, it will end up meaning nothing.

The police officer's right, and at times obligation, to use force against fellow citizens is one of the highest forms of trust the public bestows on us, and it's given in recognition that there are circumstances when the only way to eliminate a threat is through force. And yes, when that force is misused, it's a terrible betrayal of the public trust.

But it's also a terrible betrayal when force isn't used when it's needed. Think of the school resource officer at Stoneman Douglas High School in Parkland, Florida, who failed to use force. Seventeen young lives were lost as a result. Seventeen. Or the cops at Robb Elementary School in Uvalde, Texas. Twenty-two people were killed, nineteen of them little kids.

We cannot make the use of force such a minefield of second-guessing and after-the-fact judgment and flat-out unwillingness to allow for human error that officers will no longer be capable of using this force when it's needed.

Every day, whether we like it or not, there are situations where force is needed, and every day the use of force saves a life.

Every. Day.

It's easy for you to forget.

Those small incidents of necessary force don't make the nightly news, don't get written about in editorials or memorialized in poems, don't get noticed at all, and maybe never will, until the time comes when they're used against us, proof of everything that's wrong with police in America.

*Every day, every shift, tests a cop's boundaries between the man he wants
to be and the officer of the law he's required to be.*
— Blurb for the novel *Green Sun*, Kent Anderson

33

Apology to the Woman I Put in Danger When I Failed to Use Force

Late February. It was near the end of a twelve-hour shift. I received a call about a disturbance at a convenience store. A Black female was knocking over displays, screaming obscenities, assaulting customers and staff. When I arrived, I saw garbage cans kicked over in the parking lot and trash strewn about. The clerk said that after the woman finished her rampage, she assaulted another woman entering the store. The clerk had wanted to lock the doors, but was afraid for customers who might get stuck out there. She told me the woman left in a blue and white van — your van — and pointed toward the drawbridge leading out of town.

A half mile up the road another officer spotted your van parked haphazardly across the entrance of a partially lit strip mall. The van's front and side doors were open with a young Black woman sitting in the passenger seat, screaming and cursing. You and a White man stood several yards away. Do you remember this? It was already dark, one of those clear nights with the kind of bitter cold that makes the stars look like chips of glimmering steel. I remember staring up at those stars and taking a deep breath. I was bone-tired and, until the call came in from dispatch, was just counting the minutes until I could go home. Now, all I could think was *Fuck, fuck, fuck.* This was going to be a shit show.

As I approached, the man you were with stood in the shadows. He wouldn't make eye contact, so I turned to you, and felt a flood of gratitude. I knew you. Or I knew of you. *Thank God*, I thought. You run a halfway house for recovering addicts and inmates recently released from prison, and you're well-respected in police circles.

You explained that the woman in the van had just been released from prison and was staying in your halfway house. You'd dropped her off at her job several hours earlier and came to get her when her shift was over. By then, the woman was out-of-her-mind drunk and combative.

My instinct was to send her back to your halfway house, let her sleep it off, deal with the crimes committed at the convenience store once the woman sobered up. I was so damn tired, it was cold, and the clerk didn't appear all that eager to press charges. But you were reluctant. You told me the woman needed help you just couldn't give. I didn't want to hear that, but I knew you were right. This wasn't up to you.

I realized I'd have to take the woman into custody and asked her to get out of the van. As soon as she stood, she fell. I got her to a curb and sat her there while my partner did a "wanted search" on the computer in his car. He wasn't paying attention to me or my new prisoner and didn't notice her jump up and begin running. She was fast, but so drunk that every twenty yards or so she'd stumble and fall, allowing me to catch up to her. As soon as I did, she started thrashing around, landing a hard kick to my knee, to my groin.

For most of my career, I wouldn't have thought twice about promptly ending the assault by grabbing the woman, taking her to the ground, and subduing her with my weight on her back while I cuffed her. I'm a large man, but I'm trained to do this and I've had to numerous times. I have never, in over twenty years, been accused of using force inappropriately.

But this time I didn't do what I'd been trained to do. This time my safety became secondary to my fear that somehow, some-where, someone was recording this encounter, and only the most unflattering parts of it would be posted online: I'd become another racist cop abusing an innocent unarmed Black woman.

So, I tried to reason with the woman. I wasn't sure how long, but long enough for her to punch me in the face and chest, long enough to land several more kicks to my legs.

And then you grabbed her.

You threw her down and sat on her while I got the cuffs on.

You then helped me load her into my police car even as the woman continued to kick, squirm, try to bite me. Jesus, I was furious with myself. What the hell was I doing? You could have been injured because I was suddenly afraid of what the public might think about a potential video?

But it wasn't just the potential video. It was the constant second-guessing, the assumption that cops are assholes, and if we were using force and it looked excessive, it was. End of story. And would my administration back me up if there were some sort of outcry, even a measly complaint made against me? No. I'd be the one questioned. I'd be the one subjected to an internal investigation, where yeah, I could bring my lawyer, except I didn't have one — I'd never needed one.

I sat at my kitchen table for a long time that night, thinking about the incident. I wasn't happy. I couldn't believe I'd allowed myself to continue to be assaulted after the first kick. It was unacceptable. If I'd just taken care of it like I always had — quick, down, cuff, done — everyone would have been safe.

And yet I knew this would probably happen again. I'd hesitate to use force even when it was necessary. It's inevitable in this environment where any officer who uses force against any one — but especially a Black person, and God help me, a Black woman — is tried and sentenced before he gets home from his shift that night.

Still, it unsettled me. It still does. Which is why I'm writing to you now. Because in my hesitation, I didn't, for the first time in my career, live up to the oath I swear by as a police officer. Instead of doing the job that twenty years of experience taught me to do well, I was filled with doubt and I weighed the odds: Did I want to get through this shift without the potential scrutiny and second-guessing that might come from forcibly subduing the woman?

Yes.

Did I want to avoid the threat to my livelihood, possibly my freedom, should the encounter go viral and be misconstrued?

Of course.

But in choosing one kind of safety, I risked my own, as well as yours.

And I'm sorry for that.

People call the cops as if calling on God, believing in a force that is bigger and stronger than the individual, one that enforces some sort of universal law, moral reason, or code of conduct. But what arrives when people call the cops? An individual with his own deep faults and biases. We call the cops looking for some way to rein in our fear without ever examining what it is we are afraid of.
— *The Unwritten Book: An Investigation*, Samantha Hunt

34

Letter to a Young Cop About a Cop's Use of Force

The light in emergency rooms is always the same: bright with a greenish tint. Why the greenish tint?

Concerned faces pop into view. The staccato rhythm of monitors plays around the room like background music from a scene in a medical drama on TV. But it's not a TV drama. It's my real-life drama.

I'm hyperventilating. I can't stop.

"Slow it down, man. You've got to slow it down," the ER doctor says.

I'm not sure why I'm here, but the music is comforting. There's a priest next to me, his expression is solemn, concerned. Why is he here?

"What is your religion, my son?" he asks.

"I'm not sure," I say. "Why?"

And then I black out — *ketoacidosis*.

Surrounded by World War II veterans, I'm in a bed on a ward in a military hospital at Fort Lewis, Washington. It's early 1982. Most of these veterans are in their late fifties to early seventies, and they're suffering from the habits and hazards of their time: smoking, cocktails at five, steak every night — and the poisons of working in heavy industry. They are pipe-fitters, welders, foundrymen. Many are dying, but these are some tough hard men. I respect them.

The old guy next to me asks, "You a Navy guy?"

I've got a beard. Navy guys could have a beard at one time. "No," I say. We leave it at that.

A nurse comes in and tells me it's time to learn how to inject insulin — my life from now until the end. I've got juvenile diabetes.

How is force judged? Since the 1989 Supreme Court decision in *Graham v. Connor*, questions regarding the excessive use of force by police officers are measured by this ruling. In this case, Mr. Graham suffered from juvenile diabetes. A lot of people know that diabetes fucks with your sugar levels, but with juvenile diabetes, there's a greater risk of low blood sugar, or insulin shock. And insulin shock looks a lot like intoxication: slurred speech, confusion, stumbling gait, and erratic, even volatile, mood swings.

Mr. Graham realized he was suffering from insulin shock and got a friend to drive him to a convenience store. He needed to buy something quickly to raise his blood sugar (orange juice, a Coke, a pack of M&M's — anything). When your sugar starts dumping, you don't have a lot of time. You're basically being poisoned by the insulin, and it's frightening because you can go from feeling fine to being so disoriented you're not sure what's happening. The next step is often a complete blackout. Sugar counteracts the poisoning. But when Mr. Graham entered the store that day, he realized the line of customers was too long. He needed sugar immediately, and so ran out of the store and told his friend to drive him somewhere else.

Officer Connor observed Mr. Graham run from the store and jump into his friend's car. It seemed suspicious, this guy dashing inside, then frantically running out, the car racing away. So, Officer Connor followed the car. His suspicions were enough for him to stop the vehicle and make inquiries about what he'd just witnessed. In the process, Graham was handcuffed. I wasn't there, but I suspect that as his blood sugar was dumping, he was getting agitated and belligerent. Maybe to the cop he seemed violent and threatening. Maybe he was.

Officer Connor used force to subdue Mr. Graham.

I know from my own experience that when I'm going into insulin shock, I start sweating, have trouble walking, see black spots, can't articulate my thoughts even when my wife is asking the simple question, "Are you okay?" A few times I've started hallucinating and once, my wife told me, when she asked what was wrong, I started roaring at the top of my lungs. Though I don't feel physical pain, walking a short distance feels impossible as I concentrate on simply lifting my feet, setting them back down, remembering to breathe, trying to hold onto the earth. Consuming sugar will dissipate these symptoms rapidly, but that day in 1989, Mr. Graham didn't have any sugar, and he was too out of it to explain what was happening.

He subsequently filed suit against Officer Connor for excessive force.

What the court decided was that although Officer Connor was mistaken in his arrest of Mr. Graham, his use of force in detaining him was not malicious or excessive if judged by a standard of "objective reasonableness."

Reasonableness.

There's that word again.

What it means is that excessive force is judged by the reasonableness of the officer's actions based on what he perceives in that particular place and at that particular time.

A man dashes frantically into a convenience store, comes running out two minutes later, and the car he jumps in squeals away. It was reasonable for Officer Connor to find that suspicious.

Reasonableness cannot be determined by someone looking back at the event (hindsight is 20/20). Two days later — hell, two hours later — when Officer Connor understood what insulin shock was, he most likely would have made completely different choices. Perhaps he would have reached into his own lunchbox and offered Graham his Coke, as I've done more than once when dealing with someone with low blood sugar. And had I been the officer on the scene that day, an officer who understood all too well what insulin shock can do to a person, there would have been nothing reasonable about my acting as Officer Connor did.

As you can imagine, there are an infinite number of factors that determine what's reasonable in any given incident. For instance, if an officer with two years of experience makes a questionable call, it can't be judged on the basis of what his superior with ten years of experience would have done. It just can't. Instead, the questionable call needs to be looked at in terms of how other officers, also with two years of experience, would have acted.

The same holds true for an officer's level of training. You might have a rookie cop with just three years on the job, but he's a veteran; he's got combat experience and he's part of the firearms unit. He's had extensive training with pop-up targets where he has to, in the split second prior to shooting, identify if the target is a victim or villain. Maybe he's got only three years on the job, but it wouldn't be reasonable to compare his actions in a use-of-force situation with the actions of a cop like me, who has two decades on the job but has rarely had to draw his gun.

These are just two examples, based on experience and training, but there are an infinite number of factors that must be considered. It starts with the officer's perception of the immediacy and severity of the threat to herself and others, the seriousness of the offense, the risk posed if the subject escapes. Quickly, within seconds, the officer also has to evaluate the suspect's behavior: Does he have a firearm or another weapon, are his fists clenched, is he shouting or cursing, making threats, getting closer even as you yell for him to stand back? Is he mentally disturbed, in shock, intoxicated, amped on steroids? Hell, could it be insulin shock? Does he just need a damn candy bar?

And what about the physical difference between the subject and the officer: Is the suspect lanky and muscular, bouncing on his toes like a boxer, and the officer older, less agile? Is the officer fatigued, at the end of a twelve-hour night shift, or who knows? Maybe he's just started his day but he's already had a foot pursuit with a juvenile, then gave CPR to a heart attack victim, and now this. There's been no time to catch a breath, and there's not going to be.

Does the officer know backup is en route or does she feel like she's on her own? Has the officer had prior contact with the subject and was it confrontational; if so, she can't help but factor that into her response. Why wouldn't she? But another officer with the same experience, same training, same physical build who was on the same earlier calls (same foot pursuit, same CPR call), that same everything who hasn't had prior experience with the suspect might have a completely different response. All of it matters. All of it determines what is reasonable.

It's not a simple equation.

It's never one thing.

And even as the officer is making an assessment, trying to figure out how to act (and this is happening in minutes, probably less), the factors keep changing. Now there's a crowd and people are shouting and she can't tell if they're hostile or not. The light is bad and it's getting darker, and the suspect won't stay back . . .

The America I saw in the fall of 2021 was weary and battle-scarred . . . In one stop after another, I'd head to a store or a restaurant I remembered and find it boarded up, or maybe burned out, the plywood that blocked the doors covered with graffiti: "BLACK LIVES MATTER." "EAT THE RICH." "FUCK THE POLICE."

"Lucky-Go-Happy," David Sedaris

35

Letter to the Young Father Who Sheltered in My Town During COVID

It's hard to forget those early days of the pandemic, my last days as a full-time cop, when we were given direct orders to NOT respond to any calls unless there was a crime in progress or it was a priority.

March of that year was very different than other Marches I remember, the days cast in gray, homes and businesses shuttered. Ironically, in my state, liquor stores were deemed essential for the safety of alcoholics who might suffer seizures from immediate withdrawal, but Alcoholics Anonymous couldn't have group meetings for fear of spreading the disease. None of this made sense to me. My mood was as bleak as the weather. My town felt like some post-apocalyptic movie scene. Normally March was the time of spring breaks, hotels and restaurants opening for the season, and on warm days, crowds of people swarming our beach and boardwalk. I loved that time of year, chatting with store owners as they readied for the summer season, greeting visitors on the boardwalk.

Now, my sole job, on orders from the police chief, was to stop and interrogate anyone driving a vehicle with an out-of-state license plate. At one point, the chief even had a patrol car, lights flashing, guarding the entrance to our town.

When we stopped those with those out of state plates, we informed them that it was mandatory they sequester indoors for fourteen days before going out, but basically what we were really saying was "we don't want you here." Not only did it piss off the people we were stopping, but it pissed us off, too. We were potentially being exposed — and possibly exposing our families — by this unneeded contact with the public. And to what end? The whole thing was ugly, and I hated every minute of it. Neighbors were now calling the police to snitch on those who might have violated the order by going out to buy groceries. Groceries, for God's sake.

On April 1, I received an e-mail from the chief to drop by the address where people from New York — you — were renting a house. I was to inform you of the mandated quarantine for out-of-state visitors. Jesus, I thought, wishing so much that this was an April Fool's joke. You probably wished this too. All I know was that I was embarrassed to go to this call. I felt like an intruder. And sure, I go where I'm not wanted or welcome all the time — breaking up a loud party, for instance — but my reasons for showing up are solid. The party-goers are disturbing their neighbors' peace, and my task is clearly-defined, prompted by unlawful behavior. But that day? My only purpose for arriving at your doorstep was to inform you that you could not leave your house, that you were basically under house arrest. And for what crime?

In more than twenty years of service, I'd never been this conflicted about my job and its purpose. But during those early months of COVID, I felt a tide turning in me, an undertow of discomfort. This was not who I wanted to be, not how I interacted with visitors. I was the guy typically saying things like, "Hey, welcome to our town," and "Is there anything I can do for you? Let me know," and "Have a pleasant stay." And if I were responding to a domestic dispute or a drunk and disorderly, I was the problem-solver. Granted, those involved might not like my solutions, but I always found one. When I left the scene, the situation was resolved. Now, though, now I was invading your lives, and you didn't need my help and didn't ask for my presence. I'd become the messenger for your frightened, and at times paranoid, neighbors. Fear can be toxic, I learned that spring, turning otherwise good, generous, decent people ugly.

That ugliness seeped inside of me that day I came to your home.

Just a few nights before I'd appeared at your door, I'd read an article about the Black Death in 1604. The physician Paracelsus had complained in his medical manual:

> [W]hat a madness and cruel foolishness is this, that in the time of any great plague, such as are infected, you shut up in houses, set marks upon them, keep them in prison, strangle them with cares and solitariness, and kill them for hunger: is the plague so to be cured?

What madness and cruel foolishness, indeed? I remember thinking as I headed through the deserted, shuttered town toward your address.

Bottom line, I didn't feel good carrying out these orders. I believe in the rights of our law-abiding citizens to make their own decisions as long as they're legal. My job is to protect those rights, and this . . . this wasn't doing that. You had a right to be here.

But it was a direct order from the chief, which means it didn't matter how I felt about it.

That April morning, I pulled my cruiser onto the shoulder of the road across from the house where you were staying. It's one of only three streets that can be used to exit town and was usually busy with traffic. That day, like many of the days during the COVID-19 lockdowns, I scarcely saw a car driving by.

When I exited my car, the door closed with a muffled pop, like the sound that might be made when firing a bullet through a silencer. A biting wind blew as I approached your clapboard ranch house with faded shingles and dull green shutters.

The cold sank into my bones.

You came to the door. You looked to be in your mid-thirties and told me you'd come from Twenty-Third Street, New York City, the epicenter of the virus. You had a sophisticated air about you, but you weren't pretentious, only scared, seeking shelter for yourself, your wife and two small children. You were doing what a husband and father should do, I thought, protecting your family. You told me you were aware of the quarantine, that your family had already been quarantined for five days, and would continue for nine more.

Later that day as I passed your residence, I saw two small girls jumping rope on the porch. Their giggles echoed, then erupted into joyous shrieks, and I was struck by the realization that they weren't shouldering any of the burdens you or I were, that, in this moment, they were utterly carefree, unaware of the fear their being here had created in our town. I watched as those children played peacefully together as mine had done in the not-so-distant past. Again, I felt a hollowness of spirit about who I was, about the job I was doing, and again, I thought of words from centuries ago, that other time of plague: in 1625, poet George Wither wrote:

So when our Sickness, and our Poverty
Had greater wants than we could well supply;
Strict Orders did but more enrage our grief,
And hinder in accomplishing relief.

That line echoed: *Strict Orders did but more enrage our grief.*

I thought of those words often in the following weeks, weeks spent not enforcing traffic laws or stopping drunk drivers or conducting drug investigations, not even going to medical calls unless they were a life-threatening emergency because we were ordered not to. The prohibition on medical calls was the most disheartening because our elderly population relies on the police to help with small things like getting them up when they'd fallen out of bed or had too much to drink. But the only calls we were allowed to respond to were priority calls like in-progress assaults. My real job — my only job — was to enforce the emergency orders.

Increasingly, I noticed that the property owners in town, many of whom were from out of state, paid taxes, and had every right to shelter in their second homes, were backing their cars into their driveways so their New York or Maryland or Pennsylvania license plates couldn't be seen. "I own property in Delaware!" said handwritten signs taped in the back windows of cars with Maryland or Pennsylvania tags. "Stop Harassing Me!"

I hated that I was one of those who was doing the harassing.

The town, the days themselves, were so austere. Even the beach was off-limits to the public, the boardwalk barren except for the line of orange barrels blocking every entrance. The only movement came from the blinking highway signs telling all who approached that the beach and boardwalk were closed. For hours I'd sit in my cruiser at the entrance of the boardwalk like the lone survivor of some catastrophe. I was a reminder to any that approached that the enforcement was real. I was ordered to arrest anyone who walked on this otherwise deserted area.

Again, it made no sense. What danger was there in walking on an empty beach?

Strict Orders did but more enrage our grief.

As April moved into May, I began seeing banners posted across storefronts with "OPEN OUR BEACHES!" printed on them. Even normally law-abiding citizens were disregarding the mandates, jumping over barricades to walk on an otherwise abandoned beach. I couldn't blame them.

I felt the tension everywhere, the fear, the anger.

Numerous people voiced their rage at me. I had taken a vow to support and enforce the constitution, which I wasn't doing, they told me. I should be ashamed. And maybe I was a little. I agreed with those people; I, too, resented the laws. I couldn't even go surfing on my days off and couldn't begin to fathom how this protected the public. I came home from those twelve-hour shifts, and though I had done nothing, interacted with hardly anyone, I was drained, my spirit sunk. I felt I had lost my purpose as an officer. This wasn't who I wanted to be.

But this was my job, and the orders I was carrying out were not unlawful. Sure, some of the laws mandated during that strange spring of COVID-19 were not well-thought-out, but although they were done in haste, they weren't ill-conceived or malicious. There was so much fear and panic, so little reliable information — it was all too new — and the governor had the authority to declare a state of emergency. Some argued that his powers did not extend indefinitely without congressional approval, but that was for others to decide.

On that April day when the chief asked me to go to the house where your young family had fled to from New York, he was making a call based on what he thought best for his community at that specific moment.

Still, it pains me to imagine how you must have felt seeing a uniformed police officer on your porch that day. I hope I spoke with kindness and care. I think I did. And just as I understood that you were doing exactly what you needed to do as a husband and father, I'd like to believe, that if you think of me at all, you understand that I was simply doing exactly what I needed to do as a police officer.

We were both doing our jobs.

While my colleagues in the Ivy League continue to produce papers about "defunding the police," the overwhelming majority of Black Americans are clear, according to one Gallup survey from 2020: It found that more than 80 percent either want the same police presence or more police presence.
— Review of *We Have Never Been Woke* by Musa al-Gharbi in *The Washington Post*, October 14, 2024, Adam Szetela

36

Letter to the Church Ladies

During those months of massive calls for defunding, riots against the police in numerous cities, protestors in Seattle burning a police station, burning police cars, and cops being assaulted simply for being a cop, I became accustomed, as many of us did, to people (mostly college kids who have probably never had any interaction with the police) screaming expletives at me or standing on hotel balconies, giving me the finger, and more than once, approaching my window as I was sitting in my patrol car and yelling, "Fuck you, cop!"

In Tana French's novel, *The Searcher*, a kid asks a retired Chicago cop if he was mad at how so many treated the police as villains. "Not mad," the retired detective says. "Weary. Bone weary. Every day I went to the job feeling as if I had the flu and had to climb a mountain."

That's how I felt.

And then one day in September, I was parked with my window down at an intersection where the traffic often slowed to a crawl. The day was hot and the sun bright when a newer-model sedan pulled up next to me. In the front seats were two middle-aged Black men, each in a dark suit with starched white shirts and power ties. In the back were two middle-aged Black women — you. You reminded me of women when I was growing up who dressed for church as if going to a grand event: Your hair beautifully done, makeup exquisite, flower print dresses, and wide-brimmed hats ringed with bright scarves. When I described you to my wife later that night, I called you "the church ladies," which is how I still think of you.

That day, the car stopped next to my police cruiser, and the windows came down, and I felt the tension slam over me. But you were smiling. The woman in the back seat closest to my window said, "Hi, officer, we're visiting from North Carolina, but we'd like to thank you for the work you do and the sacrifices you and the other officers make for us. Know that we support the police."

And then you drove on.

Thank you.

What more can I say?

Thank you.

In police work, just like in life, "what ifs" don't really pertain.
— Anything You Say Can and Will Be Used Against You,
Laurie Lynn Drummond

37

Letter to a Young Cop About the Chain of Command

It's easy to second-guess if you weren't there, easy to decide as so many did after George Floyd was murdered by that asshole cop, Derek Chauvin, that the rookies who were with him that day should have spoken up, should have told their superior that what he was doing was wrong, should have refused to follow the order!

Should have. It angers me every time I hear it.

To defy a direct order from a superior — or worse, to tell a superior that what he's doing is wrong — is rarely done, 99.9 percent of the time for good reason, because 99.9 percent of the time, the orders we are given are lawful. Even if we don't like those orders, even if they don't make sense to us, there's often a reason — a damn good reason — they were given.

An example: On my last weekend of full-time police work, the entire department was commanded to be on hand for a demonstration against the COVID-19 mandates. Rumors had it that the protesters were armed, that gun violence was a real possibility. Many shops and restaurants boarded up their windows in preparation.

On the day of the demonstration, the protesters refused to comply with orders to wear masks and be socially distant. For months we'd been enforcing the mandates, and ordinary citizens who wanted to run on the beach or stroll the empty boardwalk had been fined for violating these orders. And it was a hefty fine, mind you, a couple hundred bucks. Now, suddenly, we were being told to stand down, to not enforce the mandates, though they were still in place. How was that fair? It wasn't and I didn't like it one bit. But the chief did this because he didn't want to amp up the anger, didn't want to increase the potential for violence. On that day, in that specific situation, not enforcing the mandates offered greater public safety than enforcing them.

But let's say an officer decided to disobey the chief because he felt the law needed to be enforced. It was the law, after all! Let's say he had the best intentions: Wasn't he keeping the public safe by enforcing the mandates? Imagine him issuing citations to those protestors, those armed protestors, for not wearing masks, for not standing six feet apart. Imagine if one of those protestors resisted the citation and started a scuffle and in that scuffle, a shot was fired. Imagine the officer or the protestor or maybe an innocent civilian, a child, getting shot.

What was more important that day? Calming the anger or enforcing the mask mandate?

The police chain of command is based on the military, where communication follows a very specific path. People assume the flow of information is from the top down, as it is in the above example, but it's equally important that when information flows from the bottom up, that it too follows a very direct, very specific, path.

Another example: I caught a guy trying to break into our county's emergency communication center, located in the same complex as the police station and protected by a high chain-link fence topped with barbed wire. Normally, I wouldn't bother my chief about a random attempted break-in — we caught the guy, no big deal. But details of this situation suggested terrorist possibilities. So, I notified my chief, and he then contacted the liaison between local police and the FBI. That was his call to make, not mine. It never would have occurred to me to contact the liaison without notifying my chief. For all I knew, the chief already had information about terrorist activity in the area that I wasn't privy to — and didn't need to be privy to.

You trust — and let me say that again, you trust — that once you pass information on to your superior, he or she will analyze it and determine where it needs to go. And your superior trusts that whoever he contacts will make the next best decision, and then the next, on up the line, following the chain of command. No one second-guesses anyone, at any level. It's not only that I trusted my chief to know who to contact, but he trusted me. My position, experience, and competence allowed him to know, without doubt, that if I was calling him about an attempted break-in there was good reason. On the other hand, had one of my seasonal officers called the chief, he wouldn't have trusted the information — and why would he? The seasonal officer doesn't have the experience. The chief would have called me wanting to know why the hell a seasonal officer was phoning him?

A great example of a well-executed large-scale flow of communication up and down the chain of command occurred during the operation to kill Osama bin Laden.

From the start, when actionable intelligence was found on the hiding place of bin Laden, the success of the operation depended on it being kept secret. Even email was forbidden. Information was handwritten and delivered in person. And analysts within the NSA who were gathering communications intelligence, mapping, and photographing locations? They did so because they were ordered to do so, though they had no clue why.

For weeks, numerous highly skilled personnel in the nation's intelligence community were not aware of why they were doing certain jobs. For example, a detailed architectural model was made of the bin Laden compound so the special operators (SEAL team) who were to strike the compound could plan, mock-up the area, and practice the assault. The model builders had no clue what the building was, what its purpose was, or why they'd been tasked with building it.

No clue.

They did it anyway.

They followed orders, trusting there were good reasons as to why they'd been asked to do this work.

And just as they had to trust their superiors, so their superiors had to trust them. President Obama had to trust his advisors; the advisors had to trust the intelligence they were getting; the intelligence community had to trust those who would carry out the mission; and the SEAL team members who would actually breach the compound had to trust everything, including something as seemingly small as the accuracy of the models. One wrong detail in that model — a wall or a window where it shouldn't be — could have affected the entire outcome, might have resulted in the lives of the SEAL team.

In other words, Young Cop, you have to trust that the orders you are given are good orders; you trust that they are given by competent, honorable leaders; you also trust those in your command.

And yeah, okay, capturing a notorious international terrorist is a long way from the day-to-day operations of a small-town police agency. I'm not comparing them. But I am suggesting that the chain-of-command is a tried-and-true organizational model that has worked for thousands of years and in dire life-or-death situations. Why wouldn't you assume it would work for you?

In two decades of police work, I have never had to defy an order nor have I ever had a subordinate defy an order I have given. It's beyond rare.

I've seen it happen just once . . .

His mother had been dead for two years when George Floyd called out for her as he was being lynched. Lynching is defined as a killing committed by a mob. I call the four police officers who arrested him a mob.
— *The Trayvon Generation*, Elizabeth Alexander

38

Letter to the Officer Who Refused to Follow a Direct Order

You are the exception, the one officer who defied a direct order, and though you were absolutely right to have done so, it ultimately cost you your job. That will always pain me because you were a great cop. I think I gave up on policework for a while after you were fired. It was hard to care, hard to believe in anymore. I ended up retiring from the agency that fired you, and although I'd been thinking about retiring for a while, what happened to you certainly sped up my own decision. I was disillusioned and maybe a little broken. It was one thing for the public to turn on us — and they had — but our own administration?

One of the things that made you such a great cop and one of the things I always admired about you was that you would never bend into gray areas to facilitate an arrest. Even when you knew with absolute certainty that someone was guilty of a crime, if you lacked sufficient evidence, you'd cut the person loose rather than find some dubious or roundabout way to make the arrest.

I respected this.

I respected you.

For a short time when I was a sergeant, our department implemented a "point system" to determine how productive its officers were. You got a point for giving a warning, two points for a traffic ticket, points for a criminal arrest (with more points assigned for a felony than a misdemeanor). Bonus points for drug or firearms arrests. There were also points for checking properties, which meant making sure water pipes weren't broken in the winter or windows and doors weren't ajar. The reason for these property checks was to identify homes or businesses, often left vacant in the winter, that were unsecure and vulnerable. In theory, this was a great service to the community, and over the years, a number of residents thanked me for performing these checks when they saw me walking around the yard of a neighbor's empty house.

Your sergeant wanted his shift to be number one in points every month, no matter what. This would make him look good in the eyes of the administration, and looking good in the eyes of the administration was his priority. As a result, he had his officers pulling on the doors (to make sure they were secure) of all residential properties even when they looked occupied. If the doors were unlocked, he mandated his officers to briefly enter, check the interior of the house, and lock the doors upon leaving. The result? Numerous complaints from incensed property owners who were locked out of their homes while taking a walk or running simple errands.

Even before the angry calls started coming in, you refused to enter private residences simply because the doors weren't locked. When the sergeant ordered you to do as you were told or be disciplined, you still refused on the grounds that the order was unlawful.

The government has no right to enter anyone's home without permission — or a warrant. End of story.

The departmental point system disintegrated not long after this, but your sergeant never forgave you. A few years later when he was promoted and ironically, put in charge of the Professional Standards Unit, he went after you on trumped-up charges, and you were fired.

You no longer work as a cop.

I think of you often, though, in part because your story illustrates how difficult it is for subordinates to question the actions or orders of their superiors. Even when the order is blatantly unlawful, it's difficult to speak up for what is right because it goes against all the tenets of trust on which the chain of command is based. I think, too, of how, in your case, the order wasn't issued in a tense, potentially dangerous circumstance; you had the time, the clarity, and the resources to research the case law — which you did — before confronting your sergeant. But what about the situation when there is no time, where the officer is frightened or threatened or the situation is escalating? He has to follow the chain of command; he has to hope he'll be given the chance later to make things right.

I thought of you especially in that awful summer following the death of George Floyd, when the public was demanding that the officers assisting Derek Chauvin, who was convicted in Floyd's murder, be charged with aiding and abetting. Two of those officers — Thomas Lane and J. Alexander Kueng — were rookies, barely off probation. It was their fourth day on the job as full-time officers.

Fourth day.

There's no way they could have refused Chauvin's orders.

No fucking way! This was Chauvin's beat, he had years of seniority, and for all those young cops knew, he'd had prior experience with Floyd, had knowledge about him they were not privy to. It's like expecting an intern to correct an experienced surgeon in the middle of an emergency life-and-death operation. Apparently, Lane did ask, twice, "Shouldn't you turn him [Floyd] over?" and was told by Chauvin that he had the situation under control. How could they have known differently? They had no context, no experience, and Chauvin was their superior and training officer.

I find it fucking heartbreaking.

I know you do too.

They both ended up in prison. I can't imagine. I don't want to imagine.

We both know that for the public to crucify these officers for not standing up to a superior is to have no understanding of the chain of command and of how that chain of command is what allows officers to do what they do well and efficiently 99% of the time. It's what allows them to conduct themselves honorably in life-and-death situations 99% of the time. Think 9/11, think Hurricane Katrina or Sandy, think massive rioting and looting, think of the lone active shooter. Ninety-nine percent of the time the officers on the ground don't have the whole story, but they act anyway, trusting what their superiors are telling them to do.

Chauvin was a bad cop, and the responsibility for what happened is on him. He broke the fundamental and essential trust upon which the chain of command is built. And if his superiors had any knowledge that he'd behaved in this manner before, then the responsibility is also on them.

Your sergeant was also a bad cop. Nothing he did could be captured on the kind of video that goes viral, but like Chauvin, he violated a sacred trust of those under his command, as well as those over him.

You and I both know the chain of command is not just about following orders.

It's about trust.

There has never, not for one minute in American history, been peace between Black people and the police. And nothing since slavery — not Jim Crow segregation, not forced convict labor, not lynching, not restrictive covenants in housing, not being shut out of the New Deal programs like Social Security and the G.I. Bill, not massive resistance to school segregation, not the ceaseless efforts to prevent African Americans from voting — nothing has sparked the level of outrage among African Americans as when they have felt under violent attack by the police.
— *Chokehold: Policing Black Men*, Paul Butler

39

Letter to Young Black Men

I sure as hell don't need to tell you that there exists a long litany of unrest, rioting, and turmoil sparked repeatedly when the police and African Americans come into contact. Our early history as a profession has dark beginnings, and there's no way that doesn't add to our present-day problems. What do we do with the fact that policing in the United States was built on the backs of slave patrols? First established in South Carolina in 1704, these patrols were initially concerned with runaway slaves, but as the slave population continued to grow (by 1740 two-thirds of South Carolina's population was Black), and White owners increasingly feared revolts, the patrols meted out punishment indiscriminately any time a group of slaves so much as gathered. No wonder African Americans don't trust us! Think about it: South Carolina's initial Patrol Act ordered patrols "to prevent all caballings amongst negros by dispersing of them when drumming or playing."

Drumming?

Playing?

And the modern era isn't much better.

Look what happened in 1965, when the Los Angeles police made what should have been a routine traffic stop involving a Black motorist. It escalated into a fight that led to six days of rioting, thirty-four deaths and more than forty million dollars in property damage — the Watts Riots. Twenty years later, Los Angeles was rocked again after another altercation between a Black motorist and the police. I know you know this. I imagine the name Rodney King is one of the many names — along with Trayvon, Eric, Tamir, Michael, Freddie, George to name just a few — that were mentioned when your parents have "the talk" with you. It's the talk about what to do if you're ever stopped, confronted — anything! — by someone like me: a White cop.

I still see that video in my own head. Those four officers beating Rodney King with their batons during his arrest for drunk driving. And then the officers' acquittals, those five days of riots, this time resulting in more than sixty deaths, two thousand injuries, and more than a billion dollars in damage — three thousand buildings burned.

Flash-forward another twenty years, and what do we have? More riots, more destruction, more deaths. Only instead of happening decades apart, the clashes between us — followed by incendiary riots, looting, vandalism, the calling in of the National Guard, the states of emergency, and mandatory curfews — are now happening within months of each other. Ferguson, Baltimore, Cleveland, Louisville, Milwaukee, Minneapolis. The list keeps growing. Why, in modern America, is there still such dissonance between the police (regardless of the officer's race) and the Black community?

History isn't the only reason. Oh, history fuels the problems, but those problems are far more complex than any one factor.

And racism, which is so entangled with police history, isn't the only reason either, though you'd never know it from the headlines. They're designed to grab attention, fire people up, make them want to keep reading (buying more papers). And they do. In just these months during which I write this letter, I read in *US News and World Report*: "Data Show Deaths from Police Disproportionately Affect People of Color"; in *Penn Medicine News*, "Fatal Police Shootings Among Black Americans Remain High, Unchanged Since 2015"; and in the *UC Berkeley News*, "Stark Racial Bias Revealed in Police Killings of Older, Mentally Ill, Unarmed Black Men." Numerous studies bear this out: "Young Black males are twenty-one times more likely to be shot by police than their White counterparts," and "Nationwide the rate at which Black people are killed by law enforcement is three times higher than that of White people."

No wonder you despise us.

Every one of those headlines and statistics is devastating. And no, I can't imagine what reading them does to you, to your parents and wives and siblings and kids. But they're terrifying to me too. Because every time those stats and headlines get repeated, the distrust and hatred that has nowhere to go except toward violence grows that much more. It puts a knot in my stomach. Not because I don't accept the truth of these studies — I do, and I wish to God there weren't so many violent interactions between us. But there are multiple, complicated reasons why the numbers are this way. And racism on the part of the cops? Yeah, that might be a reason, but it isn't the only one. In fact, far from it.

No one wants to acknowledge this.

But you and I, Black men and cops, we have no choice. Not if things are ever going to change. And even if we disagree on everything else, we agree on that, don't we?

We want to stop dying.

Still, it's the elephant in the room: a) poor Black communities have a disproportionate number of violent crimes, and b) the majority of these crimes are committed by Black men against Black men. This isn't my opinion. It's fact. Black male teenagers between the ages of fourteen and seventeen die from shootings at more than six times the rate of White and Hispanic male teens combined, and it's not because the police are shooting them. It's because they're shooting each other, their homicide rate is ten times higher than other age groups and nationalities.

Is it racist to state this fact?

How, if we refuse to acknowledge this, can we ever change what's happening between us?

A few more facts:

Black men make up roughly 6.5 percent of the US population, but they're responsible for approximately half of all murder arrests in the United States, as well as 54 percent of robberies, 39 percent of assaults, and 41 percent of violent felonies. And okay, you might say that just because they're being arrested doesn't mean they're guilty — fair enough, but are there really that many false arrests? Let's note too, that because violent crime is mainly intraracial, Black men also comprise about 50 percent of murder victims in the United States. With these numbers, doesn't it make sense that the police are going to have significantly more interactions with Black subjects than with White, and thus, a greater potential for violence? Might that be a reason for the incommensurate number of Black deaths at the hands of police?

Not racism?

Isn't it at least possible?

Or am I not allowed to ask that question either?

In Washington, DC, the cops rely on a gunfire detection system called Shotspotter, which uses audio sensors to detect gunfire. The system is linked directly to police dispatch. As one officer explains, "When Shotspotter sends out an alert for sounds of gunshots, we go where the gunshots are. How is that racist? Shotspotter can't tell the color of the person firing the gun. What should we do? Ignore the 911 calls coming from Black neighborhoods because if we go we might have to arrest Black people? The people calling 911 are Black too. Don't Black people have the right to have us come when they call?"

You insist that the issue of Black-on-Black crime is a separate issue from that of police "indiscriminately" killing Black men, but how is it separate? When Black-on-Black violence occurs, who do you think responds to the crimes?

Take just one year, 2018: There were 7,407 Black homicide victims. The police killed 235 of them, which is a tiny, tiny fraction of those deaths. For the sake of argument, let's say that every one of those 235 police-inflicted deaths was racist, unfair, unjustified, flat-out wrong. How does this ridiculously small percentage — just 3 percent — of a much, much greater whole equate to systemic racism in police culture?

It doesn't.

And again, don't get me wrong. I'm not suggesting that any death is okay. What I'm suggesting is that surrounding every homicide are dozens of unique events, factors, situations, and extenuating circumstances — an entire tragic story — and to decide racism is the sole cause is to ignore all of that.

To do so is to ignore the entangled, complex, devastating reasons for this Black-on-Black violence. It is to ignore the lack of employment opportunities for young Black men, and it is to ignore substandard, overcrowded inner-city schools. It is to ignore the lack of access to medical care that leads to physical and mental illness, which, in turn, often spirals into addiction, and yes, violence. It is to ignore the breakdown of the Black family, the lack of male role models — and the role slavery had in that. And it is to ignore how all of this leads to a seemingly unbreakable and unbearable cycle. The high crime rate is a symptom of these almost insurmountable obstacles.

To blame it on a handful of racist cops is not only convenient, it's also a refusal to acknowledge the gravity and complexity of the issue.

Now that seems racist.

If we cannot end now our differences, at least we can help make the world safe for diversity.
— John F. Kennedy

40

Letter to Those Clamoring for More Diversity in Police Departments

I hear you, I do. But more than the words you utter — *we need more diversity in police departments* — I hear the underlying fear. We can't keep going like this. We can't keep having these clashes between police and Black men.

I don't know a single cop who doesn't want this too.

We've all heard the proposals: study commissions, defunding, changes in use-of-force protocols, more community policing. You name it, the proposal's out there somewhere. And I know I sound like a broken record, but until we address the real issues — racism in schools, in jobs, in housing, in health care — the anger and despair and helplessness that lead to violence and addiction and mental illness and yes, crime, are not going to go away. They're just not. Which means the police are going to continue clashing with African American males.

It also means that your solution — we have to make police departments more diverse! — is just one more pie-in-the-sky solution with very little basis in reality. Of course, greater diversity in policing is a good thing, but can we at least acknowledge that police departments are more diverse than they've ever been, and still, racial conflicts are escalating? That the percentage of minority police officers in the United States almost doubled between 1987 and 2013? In fact, until 2020, the percentage of Black officers in the Los Angeles Police Department was greater than the percentage of the Black population; now it's equal. Or take the nearly three thousand police officers in the Baltimore Police Department: More than half are minorities, with over 40 percent African American (as of 2020). And in 2015, a year before the Freddie Gray riots, four of Baltimore's top six commanders were either African American or Hispanic, and more than half of the command leadership was from minority groups. Keep in mind, too, that of the six officers actually involved in the Gray case, three were Black.

So the diversity buzzword, your big "insta-cure," isn't working.

Maybe it's because once again we're making something about race that isn't.

The Freddie Gray case, which sparked the Baltimore Riots in 2015 after Gray died of a spinal cord injury while in police custody, is a good example. It's too easy to assume race was the issue, when we have no clue how any of the six officers who interacted with Freddie the day of his death even felt about race. The officers were charged with not buckling Gray securely in the police van following his arrest, then driving erratically, and when Gray fell, delaying medical treatment when it was clear he needed it. But we also don't know what incidents those officers had come from earlier that day, that week, that month; we don't know what was happening in their personal lives, what kind of politics they were dealing with at work. We don't know if they'd had prior experience with Freddie Gray, or what dynamic existed between the six of them as colleagues. I'm not suggesting that these other factors — if they even were factors — made what happened to Gray okay. But I am suggesting that we have no clue what else was going on and yet — and yet! — how quickly everyone rushed toward one simple, destructive answer: Gray was Black; therefore, the mistreatment stemmed from racism. Maybe it was a factor, maybe a big factor, but We. Don't. Know.

And I'm doing it too. Why am I so quick to call attention to the fact that three of the officers involved in Gray's arrest were White and three were Black? What's my point? Am I suggesting only the White cops could be racist? The Black ones couldn't be?

This isn't true either. Studies reveal that White officers are actually less prone to use deadly force against Black suspects than they are against Whites, and whether they're armed or not has no bearing.

It's too easy to make assumptions.

Look at the 2014 report denouncing the "deep-seated culture of violence" by corrections officers against juvenile inmates at Rikers Island. What do we do with the fact that two-thirds of the officers were Black? In a way, it's good, because the violence actually has to be addressed. We can't just shove it under the tidy little package of racism. We have to dig deeper into why this is occurring.

What about the Detroit Police Department, which recently emerged from eleven years of federal oversight due to patterns of alleged abuse of civilians and a history of unjustified shootings?

The department was two-thirds Black.

How about the New Orleans PD? There were so many civil rights violations that the Justice Department stepped in to try and curb the unconstitutional behavior.

Again, the majority of the officers were Black.

Making police departments more diverse, while laudable, is hardly a cure-all. In fact, some studies have found that the hiring of more minority cops shows no correlation to a reduction in the killing of citizens.

There are other proposals to try to foster trust. And I'm all for trying everything we can. Yes, officers should absolutely wear body cams to promote transparency. And of course, we can always use more training. In my state, we're required to take at least sixteen additional hours every year (though most officers I've worked with take far more training). Despite decades on the job, I continued taking classes in a vast range of subjects: negotiation techniques for first responders, law enforcement ethics, conflict management, de-escalation techniques, risk mitigation.

The more prepared we are, the safer we can keep our communities. Cops want this.

But perhaps you, the public, also needs to be educated. Not every encounter between a White officer and a Black male is motivated by race.

She was surprised when, at the end of the night, the conversation turned to race . . . even these women (frivolous, entitled) couldn't avoid the topic. It was everywhere. It was nothing new, but they spoke about it like it was. They talked about police shooting children, Black boys being murdered for walking down the street, for driving a car, for being.
— Marrying the Ketchups, Jennifer Close

41

Second Letter to Young Black Men

I feel like we're spinning in circles. Put simply, the police are dispatched to where there are calls for help. And if those calls happen to come from a minority neighborhood, and if those neighborhoods, for innumerable reasons, are rife with crime and violence, is it fair to call the increased use of force racist?

I wish I could tell you that the more experience officers have, the better their ability to react and de-escalate the violence.

God, I wish.

But, that's not the case.

We all develop expectations based on previous experience. It's why your parents have the talk with you about people like me.

But cops are no different. We've developed expectations too.

Say an officer has encountered, more than once, a suspect who refused to show his hands when told, "Let me see your hands!" Instead, the suspect reaches into his pocket and pulls out a weapon. The next time this officer commands, "Show me your hands!" and the suspect ignores this and instead, reaches for his pocket, the officer might be more inclined to fire immediately — even after the suspect pulls out a wallet and not a weapon.

Is this a reasonable response on the officer's part? Absolutely.

Is it okay? No.

But I'm not convinced it's racist either, even if the cop is White and the suspect Black. Consider that it takes four times longer to process information (*it's a wallet not a gun*) than it does to respond, and the one thing the officer doesn't have is time. Not reacting could mean the officer's life or that of a bystander. The officer does his best. In the milliseconds during which he makes a decision, the only thing he has to rely on is his experience.

And here's the thing: Just as you are apprehensive of your safety around the police, an apprehension often based on your experience or the experience of someone you know, so I'm apprehensive of my safety around you, especially in high crime areas. This too is based on my experience. But where one type of fear is deemed okay (your fear of me), the latter (my fear of you) is deemed racist.

Why?

Are we back to that crap about cops not being afraid? Not being allowed to be afraid? Well, too bad. We are. We don't run from that fear, but we sure as hell feel it. And we have good reason.

The prevailing narrative holds that right now, today, police officers are the greatest threat facing young Black men like yourself, but the truth is that young Black men, armed with guns, also pose a terrible threat to the cops. So, yeah, we're afraid and we're anxious, and these emotions set off all kinds of physical and psychological changes, decreasing everything from motor control to the ability to make a decision. When people are afraid — not just cops, but anybody — our peripheral vision is diminished, sound is altered, the ability to distinguish between relevant and irrelevant information is compromised. This too is part of the story.

And it isn't about racism.

It's about brain chemistry.

In many of those infamous videos portraying "police brutality," people are quick, almost eager, to believe that the police officer, whoever he is, shot the suspect because the cop is a racist. But maybe, just maybe, he shot because experience had taught him to be hypervigilant. Maybe, just maybe, his action, made in a fraction of a second and made with years of experience behind him, turns out to be his worst nightmare. And maybe, just maybe, the fact that he was in that home or that street or that neighborhood had nothing to do with malice or racism but everything to do with the fact that he believes with his life that every law-abiding citizen — including those in high-crime minority neighborhoods — deserve to be protected. Deserve to be protected no matter how much that cop does not want to answer that call.

Do you really think the average White cop wants to go into a minority neighborhood where he knows he's hated, where he knows he's not wanted? No. He goes because someone has to. And none of the nuance, none of the hundreds of factors that brought that specific cop and that specific Black man together at that specific moment in time can possibly be expressed in a thirty-second YouTube video or a soundbite. It's not a linear story. It's not *this happened, then this happened, then this,* even if it looks that way. It's more like *this happened, then this, and then wham!* the world turned upside down.

It's beyond frustrating. I feel like we can't win. And I know you feel that way too. I hate that we have this in common: Our fear of each other. Our distrust.

Increasingly, I find myself stepping back from situations involving men like you. Perhaps it's a drunk driver, a fight in a bar, a domestic quarrel. Are my actions racist? Or am I just practicing self-preservation? It's not that I won't stop the driver or go to the bar or show up at the quarrel, but if it looks like the situation could spiral out of control, I might overlook things that I wouldn't with a White guy. I'm not proud of this. But if things go horribly wrong with the White guy, I won't be accused of being racist, and I probably won't lose my job — and my retirement and pension that I've worked my whole life for. Oh, I'll have to defend my response, articulate why I did what I did, but my actions will be judged based on what I did, not on the color of my skin.

Look, I'm a good cop; I'm a fair man, and if I make a mistake, I know as sure as I know anything, it will be an honest mistake that happened because I'm fallible. But if I make that same mistake with a Black man, suddenly my mistake becomes a crime. Suddenly everything I've spent my life protecting is at stake.

Don't get me wrong. Will I put myself at risk if it means saving a life?

Yes. Unequivocally yes, regardless of race. I promise you this.

And will I put myself at risk if it means preventing someone from serious injury?

Again, absolutely. And I don't give a shit about race. I will step up; I will do my job.

But if we aren't talking about another life, why would I bother?

I'm not a martyr.

*I've been a policeman for over twenty-five years . . . and I'm telling you now,
they will always treat you like a dog, the people, the press, the bosses, the
politicians, regardless of whether you are black or white or brown. Unless
they're phoning you in the middle of the night saying, "there's someone at my
window" — then you're the fucking hero. But tomorrow when the sun shines,
you're nothing again. The question is: can you take it? Ask yourself
that. If you can't, drop it. Get another job.*
— Thirteen Hours, Deon Meyer

42

To the Young Officer Whose Partner Shot and Killed a Man

I can't imagine what you're feeling, because in all my years as an officer, I've never had to fire my pistol at another human being. And although you didn't pull the trigger, you were in the mix. Your partner killed a man — twenty-one years old — in part to protect you. He had no choice. You had tried to Tase the dude, but there was no cover, and he drew his pistol at you.

Now, your partner is on administrative leave, and you're gone, working for Fish and Wildlife Enforcement. It's safer there, quieter, but I just hope you didn't leave because you blamed yourself. Of course, you were scared that night. Anyone who's sane would be. Did your fear make you doubt yourself? I hope not.

The great writer Mark Twain once said, "Courage is resistance to fear, mastery of fear, not absence of fear," and he was right. Fear is normal, and there's no shame in it unless it makes you cower and walk away.

But cops don't walk away.

Not during a hurricane.

Not during 9/11.

Not during an active shooter event.

And not from a guy with a gun on what should have been an ordinary Friday night in a little beach town most people have never heard of.

Cops. Don't. Walk. Away.

You didn't and I'm proud of you.

This doesn't mean you haven't wished a thousand times you were someplace — anyplace — else when it all went down. Doesn't mean you won't feel that fear again, fear like nothing you've ever experienced before. You probably will.

Just remember that we all — and I'm not just talking cops, but everyone — have similar responses to fear. For starters, our heart rates increase exponentially, and this can result in the loss of bladder and bowel control. Our fine motor skills (finger dexterity, hand-eye coordination) deteriorate; so do our complex cognitive skills. Our sense of timing, sense of balance, ability to track and shoot a moving target greatly decrease. We get tunnel vision, able to see only what's directly before us, and we lose depth perception. We can't focus on more than one thing at a time. Ditto for hearing. Words become muffled, and we might not hear high-pitched sounds at all. Did you know that 65 percent of officers under peak stress and 89 percent of those involved in shootings reported experiencing these distortions? I'm sure you have experienced your share.

You're not alone or unique in these things. You didn't fail in your duty because you were scared that night. You didn't fall down on the job or not to rise to the occasion or any of the other bullshit clichés I suspect you started telling yourself. You fired your Taser, it didn't stop the threat, and so you sought cover. That wasn't cowardice. You were in that position because you did your duty.

And because you're a human being.

You can't respond like a robot — no feelings, no flaws, no actual physical body with a heart and lungs. Your brain responded exactly like it should have: The human body wants to survive. Don't let anyone tell you differently. Don't let anyone — not the guys on your shift who might rib you or the city's lawyer or the endless after-the-fact commentaries full of the *should haves* — make you feel ashamed because you felt fear.

You learned from this.

And if you find yourself in a similar situation, because you've already been there, you'll know now to say it to yourself: *breathe, slow down, focus.* Practice that. On a slow day at work, run some scenarios through your head and imagine how you'd react. Einstein said it: Imagination is more important than knowledge. So, imagine. Picture the traffic stop that goes to hell — the two shots fired by the driver over his left shoulder as you approach.

What will you do?

A favorite book of mine, one you should read, is called *On Combat: The Psychology and Physiology of Deadly Conflict in War and in Peace.* Author Dave Grossman writes: "Think of a warrior as a finely calibrated machine. His job is to decide in a fraction of a second exactly how much force to use. If he uses too much, he gets into trouble, and if he uses too little, he can die." This was you. It still is.

But also remember: No one is without fear unless something's seriously wrong with them.

Of course, there will be instances when you're spared the anxiety associated with fear because there's no time. Bang! It's on. I think that's what happened to you that night. One minute you're chasing a guy like you've chased down hundreds of guys and the next minute you're in a dark alley and he's raising his arm and all you can see is the gun.

You did what you had to do.

I wish the Taser had worked.

But it didn't.

Your partner did what he had to do.

I hope you're okay in your new job. You're a good cop, and I know the death of that young man haunted you. Haunts you still, maybe. I imagine it always will. Maybe it should. You witnessed a life come to an end. You were a part of that end. That's no small thing.

But don't let the fear you felt that night, the fear you might still feel, convince you that you aren't meant for this job. It's the opposite. It's only the lack of fear that would have made you unfit.

To reform the police, you need to build a healthier community where there's less need to call the police.
— "Guns Down," *The New Yorker*, April 5, 2021, program director for New Yorkers Against Gun Violence, Ian Frazier

43

Letter to the Media in the Aftermath of a Police Shooting

It has happened again. And it's devastating for everyone. But you don't help. Already questions are starting: *Why couldn't they shoot him in the leg? Jesus! They can't just use their Taser? What is with these cops and their guns? Why'd they shoot someone who only had a knife?* Or *Seriously? He had to shoot that many rounds?*

Implicit in every one of these questions, which seem more like accusations, is a judgment: Cops are trigger-happy. Well, I'm here to tell you this simply isn't true. And if you don't want to take my word, let's just look at the facts, starting with this one: Police are the target of nearly eighty thousand attacks each year, yet they use physical force or threat of force in only 2 percent of all encounters. Two percent. When was the last time you reported that? And this includes the use of all physical force, not just guns. I've been assaulted numerous times while working, but I have never, in twenty-five years of full-time patrol, fired my gun.

Never.

Except in training. Or dispatching rabid animals.

Here's a few other facts: Guns have been a part of this culture since its inception. Right now, as I write this letter, there are an estimated 423 million firearms in private circulation in America — more than one firearm for every man, woman, and child in the country, I just read in the book *Bloodbath Nation*. At least 40 percent of American households have a firearm. Some studies suggest that 35–50 percent of all civilian-owned guns in the world are in the United States.

These are facts.

Isn't that what you are supposed to be reporting?

What this means, regardless of how you or I or anyone else feels about the proliferation of guns in our country, is that right now and in the foreseeable future, the American public is an armed public. In 2014, citizens committed more than fourteen thousand murders and 1.2 million violent crimes. On average there are about one hundred gun deaths a day. Clearly, the police need to be armed, too. And the idea that we wouldn't train for the possibility of an armed confrontation — why, because there are too many guns, and guns are bad? — would be like a medic not training to deal with cardiac arrest because he thinks Americans eat too many fatty foods.

Here are two more facts:

Cops aren't paid to get killed.

We're also not paid to be seriously injured.

We are paid to deal with other people's problems, and sometimes those problems involve armed conflict. It's rare. But so is the probability of an active shooter in your child's school. Would anyone suggest we don't train for that? Would you?

Still, your questions persist: *Why not shoot him in the knee? Why so many rounds fired? Why not use a Taser or pepper spray?*

I mean no disrespect, but those questions are ignorant. Clearly, you have no clue about the magnitude of stress officers are under in any situation where a gun is drawn. And you have no understanding of the physiological impact of that stress. Our training tries to mitigate that impact by making us practice again and again and again the kind of situation where our abilities will be hampered by fear, chaos, and very little — if any — reaction time.

We're talking seconds . . . if we're lucky.

To think an officer is going to have time to clearly analyze what's going on, decide on the best weapon to use given the situation, and if he decides it's the gun, to have the luxury — and the motor skills — to determine where he wants to shoot, line up that shot, and consider the best moment to fire so he won't kill the threat but debilitate it . . . Good luck. Try doing all that in the time it takes you to say "one thousand."

It's not possible. No matter how much we train. And so, we aim for center mass.

Not someone's damn knee. Jesus. It's probably the question I'm asked more than any other: *Why couldn't they just aim for the knee?*

Along with: *But why did the officer have to fire eight shots or ten or fifteen?*

Seriously? Do people really imagine we're calmly counting our rounds, thinking, *hmmm . . . should I or shouldn't I fire one more?* In a violent confrontation, the officer has tunnel vision, impaired hearing. He's relying on his most basic instincts to Stop. The. Threat.

It's that simple.

And that devastating.

This is why we have firearms practice four times a year, both day and night shoots. We train in different light; we train in every season. If, on the day training is scheduled, the wind is howling at thirty miles an hour, it's below freezing and sleet is driving in sideways, it doesn't matter. Firearms training is NEVER canceled. It can't be. It's not like we get to pick the perfect environment for when we might need to use our weapons.

At the range we run various timed scenarios that mirror problems that might occur.

Your rifle's jammed and you can't clear it.

Transition to the pistol.

Your ammo's gone and you have to drop your magazine.

Reload as you seek cover.

Your shooting arm's injured.

Practice using your other hand; use your leg to help reload.

If we can't do this, we're not qualified to carry a firearm.

To the public, maybe to you too, this seems like a bunch of yahoos playing war games. Maybe you think we're spending too much time focusing on weapons instead of all the other things we should be focusing on. Why don't we have de-escalation training four times a year, one of your "experts" might posit. Or why not have more seminars in conflict resolution, more training in dealing with the mentally disturbed or things that might actually save a life instead of potentially taking one? More training in CPR or the use of Narcan?

Why?

Because we use these other things constantly. Conflict resolution training? It's difficult to imagine a shift where I don't use that skill: everything from arguments over parking places to domestic disputes. And the mentally disturbed? I can't count how many situations I've dealt with involving the mentally ill and their families: the girl who thought she was an octopus; the autistic man who beat his mother with a lamp; the homeless dude marching up and down the street, ranting and screaming; the vets with PTSD. It's constant. And training in Narcan? Within two days of the department being issued and taught how to use it, I saved an overdose victim from death. It's routine.

The point is that every day we work, we use these other skills. We are constantly training.

But firearms? We have mandatory firearms practice not because it's more important than anything else, but because we rarely — if ever — use our guns on the job. Where's the news report or the article in the glossy magazine on that?

I have yet to see it.

And trust me, I'm looking.

This morning, I read yet another article, this one from a well-intentioned British writer, criticizing the emphasis American police place on the use of firearms. The article happened to come from *Harper's Magazine*, but pick up almost any magazine or newspaper these days and you could find a similar commentary. Oh, they use different words, but the message is similar: American police officers are overly trained in the use of firearms. American police officers all want to emulate Wyatt Earp or Doc Holliday at the OK Corral, looking for the next gun battle. American police officers idolize the no-nonsense Clint Eastwood-Dirty Harry "Make-My-Day" type of cop, and we're schooled in the "art of killology."

Jesus. Nothing could be further from the truth. Our worst nightmare is the one where we actually have to fire our gun.

We aren't designed to take the life of another person. It damages us. It changes us.
— Bloodbath Nation, Paul Auster

44

Dear Everyone

Good cops don't want to kill anyone. Period.

If we know the names of those lost, we will remember them; if we remember them, we are compelled to fight for those that remain.
— "Loving and Losing the Natural World," Review of Lydia Millet's *We Loved It All, The Washington Post*, April 7, 2024, Caitlin Gibson

<h1 style="text-align:center">45</h1>

Letter to Lorne Ahrens, Police Officer Who Was Assassinated in Dallas

I looked for you, Lorne. I'd read somewhere that your friends called you "Meat," that you were not only a gentle giant but a gentle warrior. I didn't know this firsthand because I didn't know you or your four comrades who were gunned down on that July evening.

Although I didn't know you, I looked for you.

Almost a year and a half after you were killed, I went to Dallas to pay my respects to you, Senior Corporal Lorne Ahrens, Sergeant Michael Smith, Officer Michael Krol, and Officer Patrick Zamarripa of the Dallas Police Department, and Officer Brent Thompson of Dallas Area Rapid Transit (DART).

Before I left for Dallas, I contacted a federal agent friend who lived there to ask where exactly the assassinations had occurred. I was surprised when he said he wasn't sure; he thought it was near the police headquarters.

Then on the morning I went in search of the site, I asked a police sergeant that I saw outside of a Walmart if she could tell me where the murders had occurred. It was in downtown Dallas, she said, but couldn't tell me how to get there. "It'd probably be easier for you to just Google it."

I did, and learned it had happened on South Lamar and Main Streets, not a difficult place to find. I realized then that the sergeant probably had no idea where the carnage of her fellow brothers in blue had happened. This struck me because not only had it not been that long ago, but twice now local law enforcement didn't know where the site was. Shouldn't they have at least been familiar with the location? Why wasn't it a solemn place for them?

Driving into downtown, the weather started out sunny and warm, but when we arrived (my wife was with me) the wind had churned up, the sky was overcast, and it had gotten cold. The bus station was nearby, filled predominately with the homeless. Every variety of displaced persons seemed to be represented: the obviously insane, the drunks and drug addicts, and those who just fell off the track of life and never got back on. The area had the look of Gotham City from the old Batman comic books, gray buildings and a gray sky with wind-blown debris accenting the stark environment.

We wandered around the area and to my incredulity, anger, confusion — I'm not even sure what I felt — there was no marker, no sign, nothing, not even a Christmas wreath or a bouquet of supermarket flowers — to indicate that five dedicated police officers, loved by families and friends, were gunned down here. I wanted to weep.

Still, I looked for you.

I was able to orient myself to the scene by locating a large Bank of America sign mounted to a wall at the Bank of America Plaza. A famous Associated Press photo taken during the shootout had captured several officers seeking cover behind the sign. Picturing the scene from that photo, I was transported to the tumult and chaos of that day. If any place would be marked, it would be this site, I thought, yet sadly there was nothing.

Did anyone care?

I didn't know how to feel. I tried to tell myself that somewhere there had to be some kind of memorial, but I couldn't find it — couldn't find you.

Still, I stood at the Bank of America sign where those officers stood and fought, near where you took your last breath and I searched.

What I saw was a homeless man walking by, screaming at someone who existed only in his mind. Maybe he was talking to your ghost and the ghosts of the four other officers whose lives had been taken that day.

I thought of the officers killed in my own backyard and promised myself I would remember to appreciate any place where a cop had fallen. For me, those places are hallowed ground. Where I live, there is no marker on Kimmey Street in Georgetown where Officer Chad Spicer was murdered, but I know exactly where it is. I think of Officer Spicer every time I drive by that road. And though I've never been to the Wawa in Bear, Delaware, where Corporal Stephen Ballard was gunned down, I bet the officers who patrol that area know exactly where it is.

I hope they do.

I find comfort in this.

I felt a loneliness that day in Dallas as I said a silent prayer for you, for those other officers who died that day, for their families.

I hoped that all of us would do better — me, our families, our communities — to remember and honor those who have fallen in the line of duty.

I looked for you.

P.S. I was happy to discover that a monument titled the "Dallas Circle of Heroes Memorial" was unveiled on July 6, 2017.

The more you know about the past, the better prepared you are for the future.
— Teddy Roosevelt

46

Final Letter to a Young Cop

There are so many firsts in our history, Young Cop: Philadelphia created the first police department in the United States in 1833; Boston followed in 1838, New York in 1845. In less than fifteen years, full-time police departments were standard in all large American cities. Albany and Chicago established police departments in 1851; New Orleans and Cincinnati in 1853.

Boston was the first police department to issue guns to its police officers in 1884. The first agency to use patrol cars instead of horses was the Louisville, Kentucky, PD in 1908. The first agency to develop a police radio system was Detroit's PD in 1928.

And did you know that the practice of taking photographs of suspects began in the 1880s in New York, something still used today? Originally known as the "Rogue's Gallery," these books filled with pictures of criminals were followed by detailed descriptions that cops studied for familiarity.

Smooth shaven and wears a dark brown wig reaching over the forehead. He squints a great deal and is constantly chewing tobacco . . . prominent nose, on the left side of which are two prominent warts, stoops considerably and has a halting gait.

The first African American police officers were hired by the Los Angeles Police Department in 1886, and fingerprints were first used in a criminal investigation in 1892 to identify a woman who had murdered her two sons and cut her own throat in an attempt to place blame on another.

Believing an education was the greatest asset for a police officer to have, August Vollmer, dubbed "the father of modern law enforcement," established the Berkeley Police School in 1908. The school offered recruits courses in evidence and investigation, and at the time, was the most advanced police curriculum in the country. Volmer was truly visionary: the first to use centralized police records, establish a call box network, use motorcycles on patrol, and use a lie detector in police work.

And what about the role of women in policing? Portland, Maine, in 1878, was the first agency to allow a woman at the station (but only during the day), followed by Providence, Rhode Island, which was the first to allow a day and a night matron (called "municipal mothers"). It wasn't for another two decades, though, in 1910, that a woman was actually sworn in as an officer. In handing Alice Stebbins Wells her badge (she was not issued a uniform or baton), the chief apologized for offering a woman "so plain an insignia of office," and said "that when he had a squad of Amazons, he would ask the police commissioner to design a star edged with lace ruffles."

Lace? Ruffles?

Ummm. No.

The female officers I know would be appalled. Hell, I'm appalled! And good God, look at Wells' official duties: patrolling "penny arcades, moving picture shows, skating rinks, dance halls, and other places of public amusement, including parks on Sundays to 'perform preventive service against immorality.' " I read this to my wife and she laughed, said it reminded her of the Catholic school nuns at her eighth-grade dances, urging couples to "leave room for the Holy Ghost." The *Los Angeles Times* was so stumped by the appointment of a female officer, the paper didn't know how to refer to Wells. At first it called her "the first woman 'policeman,' " then puzzled over whether to call her an officer or an "officeress," and in later stories, referred to her as "Officerette Wells." Today, about one in eight police officers and about one in ten first-line supervisors are female.

Just as our collective history is filled with firsts, so too is my own history as a cop and so too will yours be.

My police department was founded in July 1892, with the hiring of one seasonal officer, Henry Ennis, for the months of July and August with pay "not to exceed $35 a month." One of Officer Ennis' first duties was to "take up and impound cattle and horses at large." I think of this each year when I'm training my seasonals. Remember, I tell myself on the days when the officers forget to respond to the dispatchers or forget how to use the radio or don't understand what seem to be simple commands: My department — my job — exists because of a seasonal officer.

My first dead body: I'd been a cop for just a few months. It was autumn, mid-morning and the guy, probably in his early seventies, had had a heart attack. He was lying on his living room floor — I remember the carpet was light gray, and there was an ugly yellow chair near the front door beside a table with a lamp. Why do I remember this? I can see it so clearly. Maybe focusing on that ugly chair allowed me to minimize the enormity of the task and the enormity of the consequences, for this was also my first time giving CPR. I remember thinking, this dude's life is depending on me — a guy who's never done this before.

The first time I drew my gun: I was alone, it was late at night, maybe two in the morning. I had stopped a car for a traffic violation, and the car had turned off the highway into a closed gas station. This was the olden days, when we had no computers in the car and got our info off the radio on a data channel. When I gave the dispatcher the license plate number, she told me the owner of the vehicle had felony warrants out of a nearby city. The description of the owner matched the driver. I remember thinking, there are two in the car and only one of me. I took a couple breaths, drew my gun, and ordered the driver to reach out of the window with both hands and open the door from outside.

First suicide: This particular first is always there, burned on the back of my eyelids: I've told you about it — that gunshot in the predawn darkness, that body lying limp on a small jet of sand off a lagoon near a soon-to-be-busy highway. I was a different cop after that day. Maybe that was the moment I really became a cop.

First time saving a life. Another heart attack. It was summer, and there were a lot of medical calls, no ambulances available, and to make matters worse, it was shift change. A middle-aged man had come into the lobby of the police department to make a complaint, and another officer went out to talk to him. Suddenly, I heard that officer calling over the radio, "10-40! 10-40!" a code typically used when an officer is under fire.

I ran into the lobby, where the guy was lying on the floor, bleeding out of one ear, turning purple. "Where are the medics?" I called to the dispatcher.

"At least fifteen minutes out."

So, this was my gig. The other officer started doing CPR, and someone else grabbed an AED. I'd practiced using this device on a dummy but not a human being. Another first. I attached the electrodes, administered a charge and . . . nothing. I did it again and got a pulse. By the time the medics arrived, the guy was awake, asking, "What happened?"

"Dude," I told him. "You were a dead man."

I received the Phoenix Award for this, which is given to first responders who bring someone back from imminent death. Three weeks after this event, the guy came by the station, tears filling his eyes. Wordlessly, he hugged me. Twenty-some years later, every time I put on a new uniform, I put on that Phoenix Award pin.

There are a hundred firsts, Young Cop. The first time I had to notify someone that a loved one had died. The first time I dealt with a subject who wanted to "commit suicide by cop" (he didn't). The first time I had an internal investigation against me. My first summer as a sergeant, responsible for everyone on the shift, not just myself, so that ultimately everyone's mistakes were also mine.

The first time an officer in a nearby jurisdiction was killed in the line of duty.

Chad Spicer.

September 1, 2009.

It was over a decade ago and took place in the small town that is the seat of the county. The state courts are there, red brick buildings dating back to Colonial times on a cobblestone circle. I often go there to testify and on the way to court, pass Kimmey Street, where the officer was killed. It's a seedy neighborhood street with old brick and clapboard houses, many of them sectioned into apartments. Sagging front porches with broken couches and kids' plastic toys; siding in need of paint, lawns filled with crabgrass and dirt. Before Chad was killed I'm not sure I ever noticed the street, but after, I couldn't not notice, couldn't not think about who he was and where I was on that late-summer evening when the radio was going off the charts and cops from all over the state were racing to the town to assist in finding the killer. I never knew Chad Spicer but he's a part of my history. As is the young officer, Stephen Ballard, also a cop in my state, who a few years ago was shot while making what seemed to be a routine traffic stop in the parking lot of a convenience store. How many of these routine stops do we all make? Each time another cop dies, I can't help but think how easily it could have been me.

I feel obligated to remember them, to say their names — not just Chad Spicer and Keith Heacook and Stephen Ballard, but Henry Ennis, the first officer in my agency. And Alice Stebbins Wells, August Vollner.

I think too of Nicholas Boone, that long ago constable who set out nearly three hundred years ago to do what I'm now attempting to do: convey a sense of what this job means. He and I are connected by this task we share. Perhaps, in the end, that's what history is really about — a reminder that we are not alone. What we do as police officers, who we are as police officers, is connected to all the thousands of good police officers who came before us, and all the officers, like you, Young Cop, who will come after.

NOTES ON RESEARCH

Chapter 1: Letter to the Young Cop's Well-Intentioned Family and Friends

Page 2   **Half a century ago**: Patrick V. Murphy, *Commissioner: A View from the Top of American Law Enforcement* (Simon and Schuster, 1977), 27.

Chapter 5: Letter to a Young Cop on the Anniversary of 9/11

Page 28   **James Leahy was of those officers**: Josh King, "Ten Heroic Police Officers Who Gave Their Lives on 9/11." (2013, June 29).

Page 28   **Or Officer Kenneth Tietjen**: New York Times, *Portraits 09/11/01: Collected "Portraits of Grief" from The New York Times* (Henry Holt & Company, 2003).

Page 28   **One of those daughters, Jillian**: Police1 Staff, "Daughter of NYPD Officer Killed on 9/11 Joins Force," *Police1*, April 30, 2018, https://www.police1.com/police-heroes/articles/daughter-of-nypd-officer-killed-on-911-joins-force-K3kqZBgPCYeuQu8d/.

Chapter 6: Letter to a Friend Who Didn't Trust Me as a Cop

Page 35   **Research in criminal justice finds**: Neal Trautman, *Police Work: A Career Survival Guide*, 2nd ed. (Prentice Hall, 2005), 223.

Chapter 9: Letter to the Cop Who Never Imagined He'd Become a Cop

Page 47   **It makes me laugh to read**: George Roe, "Our Police: A History of the Cincinnati Police Force from the Earliest Period Until the Present Day," in *The Role of Police in American Society: A Documentary History*, ed. Bryan Vila and Cynthia Morris (Greenwood Press, 1999), 52.

Page 48   **Let us imagine an institution**: George W. Walling, *Recollections of a New York Chief of Police* in *The Role of Police in American Society: A Documentary History*, 50.

Page 48   **Men who, before the 1929 crash:** Thomas Reppetto, *American Police, A History 1945–2012* (Enigma Books, 2012), 17.

Chapter 11: Letter to the Officer Who Showed Me the Ropes My First Night on Duty

Page 60   **It's been this way since 1833**: Larry K. Gaines and Roger Leroy Miller, *Criminal Justice in Action*, 5th ed. (Wadsworth, 2008), 106.

Chapter 14: Letter to My Wife About My Cynicism

Page 80   **As someone who had always regarded:** George Kirkham, "A Professor's Street Lessons," in *The Role of Police in American Society: A Documentary History*, 215.

Chapter 19: Letter to a Young Cop About the In-Between Ordinary

Page 115   **only a measly 2 percent:** Michael Birzer and Cliff Roberson, *Police Field Operations: Theory Meets Practice* (Pearson, 2015), 15.

Chapter 22: Letter to a Young Cop About Technology

Page 134 But reviews of technology and policing: Stephen Gies, Phelan A. Wyrick, and Eoin Healy, "Technology and Criminal Justice Policy," in *US Criminal Justice Policy*, ed. Karim Ismaili (Jones & Bartlett Learning, 2015), 293.

Page 134 When I first became a policeman: "Improvements in Police Work," in *The Role of Police in American Society: A Documentary History*.

Page 135 Dispatch data taken over the course of a year: Gaines and Miller, *Criminal Justice in Action*.

Chapter 25: Letter to My Wife About Why No One Wants Cops Around

There was something about him: Caitlin Wahrer, *The Damage* (Penguin Books, 2022)

Chapter 27: Letter to a Young Cop About the Weather

Page 162 In 1588, the Spanish Armada: Lori Cuthbert, "The Extraordinary Ways Weather Has Changed Human History," *National Geographic*, May 30, 2018, https://www.nationalgeographic.com/science/article/the-extraordinary-ways-weather-has-changed-human-history.

Page 162 George Washington and his men: Cuthbert, "Extraordinary Ways."

Page 163 Keep in mind that nine hundred officers lost their homes: Michael Peter Wigginton, Jr., "The New Orleans Police Emergency Response to Hurricane Katrina: A Case Study" (PhD diss., University of Southern Mississippi, 2007) 37.

Page 164 One officer died from an infection: Wigginton, "Emergency Response," 37.

Chapter 30: Letter to My Sister-in-Law About Our Mistakes

Page 184 Many studies, including one from the National Academy of Medicine: Kathryn Schultz, *Being Wrong: Adventures in the Margin of Error* (Ecco Press, 2011), 300.

Page 184 In contrast, American police killed, in one year (2015): Rosa Brooks, *Tangled Up In Blue: Policing the American City* (Penguin Press, 2021), 25.

Page 184 Black women are three to four times more likely: Uché Blackstock, *Legacy: A Black Physician Reckons with Racism in Medicine* (Penguin Books, 2025), 6.

Page 184 Black patients are twenty-two percent less likely: Blackstock, *Legacy*, 90.

Chapter 39: Letter to Young Black Men

Page 237 First established in South Carolina: Vila and Morris, *Role of Police*, 14.

Page 237 Patrols were to prevent all caballings: Philip L. Reichel, "Southern Slave Patrols as a Transitional Police Type," in *The Role of Police in American Society: A Documentary History*, 16.

Page 238 It escalated into a fight that led to six days: History. com Editors, "Watts Rebellion," *History*, September 28, 2017, https://www.history.com/articles/watts-riots.

Page 238 And then the officers' acquittal: History.com Editors, "Riots Erupt in Los Angeles After Police Officers Are Acquitted in Rodney King Trial," *History*, March 3, 2010, https://www.history.com/this-day-in-history/april-29/riots-erupt-in-los-angeles.

Page 238 In just these months: These headlines appeared between June and October 2020.

Page 239 Young black males are twenty-one times: John Wihbey and Leighton W. Kille, "Excessive or Reasonable Force by Police? Research on Law Enforcement and Racial Conflict," The Journalist's Resource, July 28, 2016, https://journalistsresource.org/criminal-justice/police-reasonable-force-brutality-race-research-review-statistics/.

Page 239 Nationwide the rate at which black people: Wihbey and Kille, "Excessive or Reasonable Force by Police?"

Page 239 Black male teenagers between the ages of fourteen and seventeen: Heather Mac Donald, *The War on Cops: How the New Attack on Law and Order Makes Everyone Less Safe* (Encounter Books, 2016), 30.

Page 240 Black men make up roughly 6.5% of the US population: Brooks, *Tangled Up*, 278.

Page 240 Cops rely on a gunfire detection system called Spotshotter: Brooks, *Tangled Up*, 272..

Page 240 Take just one year, 2018: Heather Mac Donald, "The Myth of Systemic Police Racism," *Wall Street Journal*, June 2, 2020.

Chapter 40: Letter to Those Clamoring for More Diversity in Police Departments

Page 246 The percentage of minority police officers in the U.S. almost doubled: Victoria Bekiempis, "The New Racial Makeup of U.S. Police Departments," *Newsweek* (2015, May 14). https://www.newsweek.com/racial-makeup-police-departments-331130

Page 246 In the Los Angeles Police Department: The decrease is a result of numerous officers, hired in the 1980s and '90s, retiring. Prior to this, the percentage of Black officers was greater than the percentage of the Black population. Kevin Rector, "Coronavirus Undercuts LAPD Recruitment Just as a Decline in Black Officers Looms," *Los Angeles Times*, May 7, 2020, https://www.yahoo.com/news/coronavirus-undercuts-lapd-recruitment-just-173211174.html.

Page 246 Or take the nearly 3,000 police officers in the Baltimore Police: These figures come from the Baltimore Police Department and were reported by Richard Pollock in the *Daily Caller* (May 14, 2015). Of the 2,745 active duty police officers in the department, 1,445 were African-American, Hispanic, Asian, or Native American.

Page 246 Keep in mind, too, that of the six officers: Photos of the Baltimore officers who were involved appear in *The New York Times* article "Baltimore Officers Will Face No Federal Charges in Death of Freddie Gray," by Rebecca Ruiz (September 12, 2017): https://www.nytimes.com/2017/09/12/us/freddie-gray-baltimore-police-federal-charges.html.

Page 247 Studies reveal that White officers are less prone: Bill Bratton and Peter Knobler, *The Profession: A Memoir of Community, Race, and the Arc of Policing in America* (Penguin Press, 2021), 369.

Page 247 Look at the 2014 report: Mac Donald, *The War on Cops*, 13.

Page 247 What about the Detroit Police Department: Mac Donald, *The War on Cops*, 13.

Page 247 How about the New Orleans PD: Mac Donald, *The War on Cops*, 13.

Page 247 In fact, some studies have found that the hiring of more minority cops: Jennifer Cobbina-Dungy, "Is Hiring More Black Officers the Key to Reducing Police Violence?," *The Conversation*, February 4, 2020, https://theconversation.com/is-hiring-more-black-officers-the-key-to-reducing-police-violence-126075.

Chapter 41: Second Letter to Young Black Men

Page 252 Consider that it takes four times longer: Audrey Honig and William Lewinski, "A Survey of the Research on Human Factors Related to Lethal Force Encounters: Implications for Law Enforcement Training, Tactics, and Testimony," *Law Enforcement Executive Forum* 17, no. 3 (2008): https://www.forcescience.com/2008/07/a-survey-of-the-research-on-human-factors-related-to-lethal-force-encounters-implications-for-law-enforcement-training-tactics-and-testimony/.

Chapter 42: To the Young Officer Whose Partner Shot and Killed a Man

Page 258 But everyone — have similar responses to fear: Darin M. Clay, "Understanding the Human Physiological and Mental Response to Critical Incidents" (presentation, School of Law Enforcement Supervision Session XVIII, Little Rock, AR, November 9, 2001), https://www.cji.

edu/wp-content/uploads/2019/04/darin_clay.pdf. Note: Numerous articles have been written on this.

Page 258 Did you know that 65 percent of officers under peak stress: Honig and Lewinski, "Survey of Research on Human Factors."

Chapter 43: Letter to the Media in the Aftermath of a Shooting

Page 263 Police are the target of nearly eighty thousand attacks each year: FBI, *Officers Killed and Assaulted in the Line of Duty, 2023 Special Report* (2023), https://cde.ucr.cjis.gov/ LATEST/resources/reports/Officers%20Killed%20and%20 Assaulted%20in%20the%20Line%20of%20Duty%2C%20 2023.pdf.

Page 263 Yet they use physical force or threat of force: Leonard Adam Sipes, Jr. "54 Million Police-Citizen Contacts — 2% Involve Force or Threat of Force." CrimeinAmerica. net. (2022, November 28). https://www.crimeinamerica. net/54-million-police-citizen-contacts-2-percent-involve-force-or-threat-of-force/

Page 264 More than one firearm for every man, woman: Paul Auster, *Bloodbath Nation.* (Grove Press, 2023), 39.

Page 264 On average there are about 100 gun deaths a day: Paul Auster, *Bloodbath Nation,* 39.

Page 266 This morning, I read yet another article: Hari Kunzru, "Another World Is Possible," *Harper's Magazine,* March 2021. https://harpers.org/archive/2021/03/ another-world-is-possible-criminal-justice-reform/

Chapter 45: Final Letter to a Young Cop

Page 281 Philadelphia created the first police department: Gary Potter. "The History of Policing in the United States, Part 1." (2013, July 30). https://www.academia.edu/43389392/The_History_of_Policing_in_the_United_States

Page 281 Boston was the first police department: Police1.Com. "Illustrated Timeline: Policing in the US: From British Institutions to Dark Blue Uniforms, Police Milestones Are Pictured and Explained." (2011, October 14). https://www.police1.com/misc-law-enforcement-topics/articles/illustrated-timeline-policing-in-the-us-DYnO0qYNazuOXtgB/

Page 281 The first agency to use patrol cars: Police1.Com. "Illustrated Timeline."

Page 281 The first agency to develop a police radio system: Police1.Com. "Illustrated Timeline."

Page 281 And fingerprints were first used: Police1.Com. "Illustrated Timeline."

Page 282 Believing an education was the greatest asset: Amy B. Thistlethwaite, and John D. Wooldredge. "Forty Studies that Changed Criminal Justice" in *Explorations into Criminal Justice Research.* (Prentice Hall, 2010), 21.

Page 282 Portland Maine, in 1878, was the first agency (to hire women): Bryan Villa and Cynthia Morris. *The Role of Police in American Society: A Documentary History.* (Greenwood Press, 1999), 55

Page 282 At first it called her "the first woman 'policeman'": The Daily Mirror Blog. (2007, August, 19). "The Vexation of Research," *Los Angeles Times.*

Page 282 Today, about one in eight police officers: Shelley S. Hyland and Elizabeth Davis. (2019, October 25). "Local Police Departments, 2016: Personnel." Bureau of Justice Statistics. https://bjs.ojp.gov/library/publications/local-police-departments-2016-personnel

ACKNOWLEDGEMENTS

This book was twenty-seven years in the making. Twenty-seven years of human interactions — the crux and essence of police work. Looking back, I realize it was the public I have served and the men and women who served with me that were the most profound inspiration for this book. With that said, there are several people whose faith in me, along with their examples of integrity and duty and their endless unselfish help, pushed me to actually attempt this project.

By far the most important person responsible for this book is my wife, Maribeth Fischer, who is a brilliant writer. She believed not only in this book but in me. Using her talents as a writer, editor, and teacher, she managed to guide me in creating a book that truly captures my commitment to letting readers see the guy behind the badge. I can never repay her.

Thanks to Maria Hess, the then-editor of *Delaware Today* magazine, who in 2013 took a chance and was the first to publish one of my essays, "Suicide by Cop." Publisher and editor Terry Plowman also published a number of my police-related essays in his magazine, *Delaware Beach Life*. The editors of *Creative Nonfiction* in 2022 published my essay, "Let's Say," giving me some national recognition. And The Delaware Division of the Arts, not once but twice, awarded me fellowships so I could pursue my writing.

I am thankful that Chief Leon McCabe of the Millsboro Police Department was the first to hire me and start me on this path. Rehoboth Beach Chief of Police Keith Banks saw potential in me and enticed me to join the Rehoboth Beach Police Department, where I served the bulk of my career. I am so grateful that Chief Sam Mackert, Lieutenant William Hocker, and my "old" surfing pal Lieutenant Cliff Dempsey persuaded me to come out of retirement and work a few more years for the Dewey Beach Police Department. I admire Chief Constance Speake for stepping in as the present Chief of Police of Dewey Beach and I'm grateful that she still encourages me to stay on as an active patrol officer (which takes a lot of courage on her part!). Thank you, as well, to all the officers I've served with in these departments and the ones from other departments who showed up when I desperately needed them.

In closing, there are three men who have had the greatest impact on how I approach police work. The first was my lead "TAC" officer during my recruit training at the Delaware State Police Academy: Dr. Joseph Aviolao, who was my sergeant at the time of my training. Although he had been Trooper of the Year and checked all the boxes of a Class A Trooper, he taught me the most important traits of the profession: duty, empathy, compassion, discipline, and fortitude.

My longest serving partner on patrol was Sergeant Curtis Sauve, a quiet, patient man who raised four daughters. He has been with me through some really scary times. He always remained cool, calm, and collected. Yet, he was not opposed to singing "Barnacle Bill the Sailor" with me to tone things down. Thank you, Curtis, for those shared times.

And finally, I'd like to thank my father, who spent his life in the service of this country. He never lost sight of life's possibilities and was not afraid to chase a dream. He made me the man I am, and he showed me the importance of family and, most importantly, duty. Thanks, Dad.

ABOUT THE AUTHOR

Victor Letonoff has over two decades of experience as a police officer and has been writing and publishing about police work for the past ten years, winning a number of national awards. In addition to two fellowships from the Delaware Division of the Arts, he has published a number of essays in Police1 and his essay, "Let's Say," was listed as notable in *Best American Essays 2023*. For more information about Victor go to victorletonoff.com

ABOUT THE PUBLISHER

The Sager Group was founded in 1984. In 2012 it was chartered as a multimedia content brand, with the intent of empowering those who create art — an umbrella beneath which makers can pursue, and profit from, their craft directly, without gatekeepers. TSG publishes books; ministers to artists and provides modest grants; and produces documentary, feature, and commercial films. By harnessing the means of production, The Sager Group helps artists help themselves. For more information, please see TheSagerGroup.net.

MORE BOOKS FROM THE SAGER GROUP

Miss Havilland: A Novel
by Gay Daly

The Orphan's Daughter: A Novel
by Jan Cherubin

Lifeboat No. 8: Surviving the Titanic
by Elizabeth Kaye

Into the River of Angels: A Novel
by George R. Wolfe

Who She Was: My Search for My Mother's Life
by Samuel G. Freedman

The Stories We Tell: Classic True Tales
by America's Greatest Women Journalists

New Stories We Tell: True Tales by America's New
Generation of Great Women Journalists

Newswomen: Twenty-Five Years of Front-Page Journalism

The Someone You're Not: True Stories of Sports, Celebrity,
Politics & Pornography by Mike Sager

What Makes Sammy Jr. Run?: Classic Celebrity Journalism Volume 1
(1960s and 1970s) edited by Alex Belth

Our Washington, DC: America's Hometown in Transition
edited by Susan Sheehan

The Dreyfus Collection: A Novel by Estelle Rubin Brager

See our entire library at TheSagerGroup.net

THE SAGER GROUP
Artifex Te Adiuva

www.ingramcontent.com/pod-product-compliance
Lightning Source LLC
Chambersburg PA
CBHW020912060726

47591CB00004B/1212